An Impulse to Soar

Quotations by Women
on Leadership

Compiled by
ROSALIE MAGGIO

PRENTICE HALL PRESS

One can never
consent to creep
when one feels
the impulse to soar.

H ELEN K ELLER

To Irene C. Maggio
loved and loving mother
who gave us the impulse to soar

Contents

v

Introduction

The words "women" and "leadership" have not, historically, been used together very often. We live now in an age in which the two terms walk hand in hand and are less and less often thought of as an odd couple.

The day we are moving toward, however, is the day we no longer need to specify a sex for "leadership," when saying the word "leader" will bring to mind both women and men, when leadership positions are as accessible to women as they are to men. We know the day is coming because here and there across the United States it has arrived.

We have an urgent need today for far-sighted, clear-headed, honest leaders. Vital leaders who can empower those around them to be leaders in their turn are the most needed of all. In 1970, Shirley Chisholm wrote, "Tremendous amounts of talent are being lost to our society just because that talent wears a skirt." We can't afford to lose leadership talent to a system that bases its judgments on sex.

In her 1924 book, *Office Etiquette for Business Women*, Ida White Parker wrote, "Women have been in business such a long time now, they have for so many years been accepted on the same terms with men, that it seems almost archaic to caution them about expecting special courtesies and favors because of their sex."

This is not the first time in history that great numbers of women have worked outside the home. Nor is it the first time in the business world that women have "been accepted on the same terms with men" or that women have written about leadership. Dale Spender says, "For centuries women have been saying many of the things we are saying today and which we have often thought of as new."

We want to keep today from being another sporadic, orphaned instance of women's gains in equality in the workplace. It is unthinkable that women in the year 2050 should be as surprised to learn what we are doing today as we are to hear that in 1924 at least some women in business had "for so many years been accepted on the same terms with men." One of the best ways of underwriting the future is sharing the lessons, the skills, the powers, the attitudes, and the hard-won advances of today's leaders.

In *Times and Places* (1970), Emily Hahn wrote, "When I read about some important moment or era in history, I always take it for granted that the people it happened to were aware of what was going on. In my mind's eye, I see the agricultural workers of England during the Industrial Revolution feeling the pinch and saying to each other, 'Eh, lad,' or whatever agricultural workers would say in those days, 'what dost tha expect? It's this Industrial Revolution at the bottom of it.' "

What we know, then, is that we want to be aware of what is happening today in the area of leadership, we want to both protect and share the good news of leadership by *all* the people, and we want to be sure that those who come after us have shoulders to stand upon.

Leadership

Leadership is one of the most enduring, universal human responsibilities.

ROSABETH MOSS KANTER

The word "leadership" is found in every language. It can be traced back at least as far as ancient Egypt. . . . In English, the word "leader" is more than 1000 years old, and little has changed from its Anglo-Saxon root *laedere*, meaning "people on a journey."

KARIN KLENKE

Our first responsibility as a leader is to create an attractive dream, to proclaim a destination, communicating it in detail to others who might be interested in joining our expedition.

SUSAN COLLINS

Leaders have to make people believe that the hard journey of change and transformation is not only urgently necessary but will lead to something worthwhile. Leaders have to inspire confidence in people who are racked by doubt.

JUDITH M. BARDWICK

The easiest definition of leadership is the ability to decide where you're going and to know how to get there.

MADELINE MARIE DANIELS

Leadership is the process by which one individual consistently exerts more impact than others on the nature and direction of group activity.

BARBARA KELLERMAN

Leaders are usually people of vision, effective communicators, effective decision makers, and intelligent; they respect and value individuals and their dignity; they are committed to service and to obedience to the unenforceable; they have total honesty and integrity; they are kind; and they often see themselves as teachers.

SARA E. MELÉNDEZ

The successful leader shares a vision of service, excellence, and achievement with others.

MARILYN MANNING AND PATRICIA HADDOCK

Leaders must (1) define the business of the business, (2) create a winning strategy, (3) communicate persuasively, (4) behave with integrity, (5) respect others, and (6) act.

JUDITH M. BARDWICK

Leadership is not for those who want an easy life or for those who want to maintain things as they are. Leadership is for those who have talents in some field of human endeavor and have a vision of how to vastly improve it. Leaders are willing champions of the revelations of creativity and the destiny of human dignity. Leaders are pathfinders to increase the common good.

SYLVIA BUSHELL

What a rope of sand we are without a leader.

MARJORIE BOWEN

Leadership is elusive and enigmatic, just as it is enlightening and empowering. It is a bright light among human energies that sometimes, by its very intensity, casts a long and dark shadow.

MARCIA LYNN WHICKER

A successful leader commits herself to her organization and fosters that same kind of commitment in her followers.

MARILYN MANNING AND PATRICIA HADDOCK

Leaders have passion and they have a picture, a picture or vision at some distance from the current reality. They use their passion to move them toward that vision, whether it's something for their company, for themselves, or for some cause.

SANDY LINVER

A good leader has a plan that consists of changing simple pictures. Just because a group of people has a bunch of boards, hammers, and nails does not mean that they are building a house or even anything recognizable. Sometimes leaders think they are doing their job just because there is a lot of hammering going on. As a society we like the sound of hammering, but we are uncomfortable with the sound of thinking, which is silence.

LAURIE BETH JONES

If you would be a leader, you must resist the reactive role that is the easier path. Those who succumb to fire fighting and crisis management will seldom enjoy the pleasures of achievement.

PRISCILLA ELFREY

The leader releases energy, unites energies, and all with the object not only of carrying out a purpose, but of creating further and larger purposes. And I do not mean here by larger purposes mergers or more branches; I speak of *larger* in the qualitative rather than the quantitative sense. I mean purposes which will include more of those fundamental values for which most of us agree we are really living.

MARY PARKER FOLLETT

Leadership . . . means understanding the job responsibility, then going one step further.

JUDY COLUMBUS

Good leadership is pervasive, persuasive, and persistent. Bad leadership is poisoned with pedanticism, posturing, self-importance.

MARCIA LYNN WHICKER

It's very difficult to evaluate a leader in a very short-term perspective because to be a leader you must be able to have a long-term perspective. You must be able to carry changes which take many years. And this is why you can really only see whether it has been a good leadership after some years have passed.

GRO HARLEM BRUNDTLAND

Rugged individualism, a cherished value in American society, can cloud our vision, causing us to forget that leaders ultimately serve others.

DELORESE AMBROSE

To some people, serving others may seem like the role of a subordinate, not a leader. But in fact, a good leader believes in service to others.

CONNIE PODESTA AND JEAN GATZ

I think that leadership is damn difficult! And, I think that it may be easier than ever to become a leader because there are fewer takers. In a recent poll, Yankelowich, Skully and White revealed that 80% of the people interviewed admitted they have been deeply affected by the new narcissism and feel that their own needs for sensation, novelty and ego-fulfillment take precedence over the needs of all other people. You sure can't feel *that* way and lead for long.

JUDY COLUMBUS

True leadership does have a strong spiritual component. Our organizations are only as good as the people who run them. Preparation for effective leadership, then, involves preparing the *soul* of the leader. We must continually examine our motives for leading. The responsibility of leadership is one of shaping our own and others' lives, hopefully for the better.

DELORESE AMBROSE

People are leaders as long as they create followers. Leadership, ultimately, is an emotional bond, sometimes even a passionate commitment between followers and the leader and his or her goals. Leadership is different from other relationships in that *leaders generate hope and conviction in followers.* They are people whom others perceive as being able to make things better.

JUDITH M. BARDWICK

Leadership is tied to *conviction.* Leaders have a vision of a better future, they feel strongly about the need to go there.

DELORESE AMBROSE

Effective management begins with the inability to leave well enough alone, with a preoccupation for betterment.

PRISCILLA ELFREY

Perhaps the true mark of a leader is that she or he is willing to stand alone.

L A U R I E   B E T H   J O N E S

To me, leadership means being called aggressive and saying "thank you."

J U D Y   C O L U M B U S

The mark of a leader may be the ability to prevent fire fighting behavior and to seek elegant solutions.

P R I S C I L L A   E L F R E Y

Leadership both projects to the future and reflects upon the past. It bursts with possibilities, flaunts peculiarities, and occasionally defies probabilities.

M A R C I A   L Y N N   W H I C K E R

Leaders seem to have a high tolerance for ambiguity. Recognizing that the brain does not work in a completely linear fashion, leaders demonstrate a comfort with the chaos of exploding ideas, many of them seemingly unrelated to the stimulus that caused them.

MARLENE CAROSELLI

We *all* come to this point at some time. . . . It is that place where you realize that leadership is a choice! That time when you take for granted that there will be risk, there will be aloneness, there will be unfinished work and stressful decision-making. That point when you ask yourself, "Who am I?" and "Who do I want to become?" "Is this move important enough to me?" And, "How ambitious am I?" If you get the right answers, go for it!

JUDY COLUMBUS

The best leader does not ask people to serve him, but the common end. The best leader has not followers, but men and women working with him.

MARY PARKER FOLLETT

We can practice leadership principles, but the only way to learn to use them is to lead. Not knowing it all is no excuse not to start.

JUDY COLUMBUS

Developing oneself as a leader takes time. If we take leadership development seriously, it occupies much of our life space across the entire lifespan.

KARIN KLENKE

Leadership is not something that you learn once and for all. It is an ever-evolving pattern of skills, talents, and ideas that grow and change as you do.

SHEILA MURRAY BETHEL

Putting a strict, presumably encompassing definition on leadership limits our thinking about the phenomenon. Moreover, the requirement that an agreed-upon definition be established hinders individuals in thinking critically and deciphering for themselves what leadership means in different situations.

KARIN KLENKE

There are few, if any, universal paths to leadership.

DELORESE AMBROSE

The true leaders—those who hold enterprises together and keep spirits high—wear no standard uniform of personality and spring from no single heritage. . . . Understanding that leaders come in all flavors and sizes frees us to contemplate our own eligibility for leadership roles.

DAYLE M. SMITH

Leaders are bridges that connect people to the future. They include others' visions in their own, building alliances and partnerships based on shared aspirations.

CAELA FARREN AND BEVERLY L. KAYE

Key to the societal significance of tomorrow's leaders is the way they embrace the totality of leadership, not just including "my organization" but reaching beyond the walls as well.

FRANCES HESSELBEIN

In most important ways, leaders of the future will need the traits and capabilities of leaders throughout history: an eye for change and a steadying hand to provide both vision and reassurance that change can be mastered, a voice that articulates the will of the group and shapes it to constructive ends, and an ability to inspire by force of personality while making others feel empowered to increase and use their own abilities.

ROSABETH MOSS KANTER

The leader beyond the millennium will not be the leader who has learned the lessons of *how to do it*, with ledgers of "hows" balanced with "its" that dissolve in the crashing changes ahead. The leader for today and the future will be focused on *how to be*— how to develop quality, character mind-set, values, principles, and courage.

FRANCES HESSELBEIN

A common theme present in most discussions of leadership for the 21st century is the leader's ability to create, articulate, and communicate not only a vision, but, more importantly, a global vision.

KARIN KLENKE

The three major challenges CEOs will face have little to do with managing the enterprise's tangible assets and everything to do with monitoring the quality of: leadership, the work force, and relationships.

FRANCES HESSELBEIN

Leaders have to create the perception that they have some significant control over the present and the future of the organization because they know where the organization can and should go.

JUDITH M. BARDWICK

Leadership development begins and ends with the internal developmental struggles of the individual leader. It is by integrating and learning from these crises that we gain the stamina and tools of effective leadership. In short, our blueprint for leadership is embedded in our own life story.

DELORESE AMBROSE

Management is aimed at *maintenance*. The effective manager ensures that organizational goals are met efficiently and profitably, with a minimal amount of disruption. . . . Leadership is aimed at *change*. The effective leader inspires and empowers others to respond to challenges by using their creativity to secure the best possible future for all concerned.

DELORESE AMBROSE

Leadership is creating a state of mind in others. The difference between being a leader and manager, all due respect to managers, is that leaders have to create states of mind. But a leader, first of all, has to have a clear state of mind, which is usually her own vision, which energizes her, motivates others, and then creates that state of mind in others.

B ARBARA M IKULSKI

Ultimately, leaders lead because they create a passionate commitment in other people to pursue the leader's strategy and succeed. In the end, leadership is not intellectual or cognitive. Leadership is emotional.

J UDITH M. B ARDWICK

Managers produce orderly results, concentrate on the short run, seek consistency, and solve problems. Leaders by contrast produce significant change, develop long-term visions, establish new directions, and produce innovative and creative opportunities. Managers thrive on order and control, while leaders embrace chaos and empowerment. Managers tend to avoid conflict, while leaders find creative value in conflict. . . . An effective balance between leadership and management is essential for organizational survival and success.

KARIN KLENKE

Great leaders make leadership look so easy.

PAT HEIM AND SUSAN K. GOLANT

Power

No issue is more central to a discussion of leadership than the subject of power.

MARILYN LODEN

Power is America's last dirty word. It is easier to talk about money—and much easier to talk about sex—than it is to talk about power.

ROSABETH MOSS KANTER

Despite the negative connotations of the word, power (or influence) is something that everyone exerts a good deal of the time. . . . It is the coercive or abusive use of power, not power itself, that we find offensive.

ANN HARRIMAN

Actually, power is like money: neither good nor bad. Its negative or positive spin depends upon how we use it.

PAT HEIM

The leader who uses power well is aware of the good uses to which it can be put; she has accepted the ramifications of using power, knowing it is necessary if she is to operate in the most efficient manner. Power is just one more vehicle to facilitate accomplishments.

MARLENE CAROSELLI

Achieving power . . . is a combination of timing, luck, and hard work. Plus one other ingredient women overlook a lot. That's wanting power.

JANE TRAHEY

The thing women have got to learn is that nobody gives you power. You just take it.

ROSEANNE BARR

Wanting power is half the secret of getting it.

JANE TRAHEY

When leadership rises to genius it has the power of transforming, of transforming experience into power. And that is what experience is for, to be made into power. The great leader creates as well as directs power.

MARY PARKER FOLLETT

Powerful people are seen as such because they have the capacity to give power to others and they do so.

ROBIN BOWMAN

You're not successful till you've helped someone else. If you want to sit up there, aloof and isolated like the Wizard of Oz, scaring everyone with fake power, you'll never move on. Lending a hand makes you feel stronger in your soul and it makes you look stronger to others.

JENNY PEREZ

When you give people power, you give them strength to make you strong.

EVELYN DUNN

Top-down leaders, by withholding power from those in the ranks, deprive them of the ability to use the expertise and information vested in them to respond directly and with speed to customer concerns.

SALLY HELGESEN

Powerlessness corrupts. Absolute powerlessness corrupts absolutely.

ROSABETH MOSS KANTER

We can confer authority; but power or capacity, no man can give or take. The manager cannot share *his* power with division superintendent or foreman or workmen, but he can give them opportunities for developing *their* power. . . . More power, not division of power, should always be our aim.

MARY PARKER FOLLETT

Ｔrue leaders have so much power they are willing to give it away. Power is not a fixed, quantifiable sum; instead it is an unlimited abstraction which grows as it is shared.

MARLENE CAROSELLI

Ｌeadership is not about power. It's about success at getting people to move with you for the good of the cause.

GWENDOLYN BAKER

Ｔhat is always our problem, not how to get control of people, but how all together we can get control of a situation.

MARY PARKER FOLLETT

Current research is showing that true leaders enjoy using their power and are comfortable with it—so comfortable, in fact, that they don't mind sharing that control when it is appropriate to do so.

MARLENE CAROSELLI

Power-over is resorted to time without number because people will not wait for the slower process of education.

MARY PARKER FOLLETT

Exert control *through* people, not *upon* them.

DAYLE M. SMITH

Coercive power is the curse of the universe; coactive power, the enrichment and advancement of every human soul.

MARY PARKER FOLLETT

Power is the ability to get things done, to mobilize resources, to get and use whatever it is that a person needs for the goals he or she is attempting to meet. In this way, a monopoly on power means that only very few have this capacity, and they prevent the majority of others from being able to act effectively. Thus, the *total* amount of power—and total system effectiveness—is restricted, even though some people seem to have a great deal of it. However, when more people are empowered—that is, allowed to have control over the conditions that make their actions possible—then more is accomplished, more gets done.

ROSABETH MOSS KANTER

Simply stated, power is the ability to get things done.

PAT HEIM AND SUSAN K. GOLANT

The degree to which the opportunity to use power effectively is granted to or withheld from individuals is one operative difference between those companies which stagnate and those which innovate.

ROSABETH MOSS KANTER

Most people do not think about their potential for power. The leader does. She is willing to use her power over others to make things happen. She extends her influence whenever she can with whatever tools she has or can borrow.

MARLENE CAROSELLI

Power is strength and the ability to see yourself through your own eyes and not through the eyes of another. It is being able to place a circle of power at your own feet and not take power from someone else's circle.

AGNES WHISTLING ELK

Personal power grows out of our integration; it is our expressed integrity. Personal power begins with our relationships with the self and then extends to our relationships with others (interpersonal power).

MARILYN J. MASON

We all have limits. A characteristic of the personally powerful person is the ability to recognize, accept, and respect those limits.

MARY ELIZABETH SCHLAYER

Personal power, which is derived from our ability to act in the interest of ourselves and others, is developed from our ability to first clearly see and understand ourselves.

JILL JANOV

Y̶ou develop a sense of personal power by developing authority, accessibility, assertiveness, a positive image, and solid communication habits.

MARILYN MANNING AND PATRICIA HADDOCK

P̶ersonal power is derived from three attributes: credibility, integrity, and trust. Each of these is an outcome of our words and deeds. Each is earned in the moment, each is created over a lifetime, and each is a hallmark of our character insofar as we are consistent in our actions. Our reputation can be obliterated in the blink of an eye. We bank our credibility, integrity, and trust in successive interactions and transactions with others. For many the account is low. For some it does not exist. For others, the account has been emptied. Whether the account is depleted or building, it is only as full as the last transaction.

JILL JANOV

How we use power and which forms of power we use create our reputations. Our reputations are critical to our success. They are determined not only by our behavior but by the subtle and not so subtle strategies we use, including whether we present a nonthreatening image, align with powerful others, develop liaisons, use trade-offs, and diffuse opposition. Our reputations, more than anything else, determine the degree of personal power we have.

JILL JANOV

The end point of leadership is not just the position of power we reach, but the continual change and deepening we experience that makes a difference in our lives, our work, our world. Our leadership journeys are only at *midpoint* when we have achieved a position of power.

JANET O. HAGBERG

Team-Building

The leader is one who can organize the experience of the group . . . and thus get the full power of the group. The leader makes the team. This is preeminently the leadership quality—the ability to organize all the forces there are in an enterprise and make them serve a common purpose.

MARY PARKER FOLLETT

People will support that which they help to create.

MARY KAY ASH

33

What I've learned is that if people understand what needs to be done, almost anything can be accomplished.

MARILYN MARKS

Any group has a sense of who it is and what it values, but this sense often remains beneath the surface. A wise leader can discern these unspoken beliefs and articulate them.

DIANE DREHER

In crowds we have unison, in groups harmony. We want the single voice but not the single note; that is the secret of the group.

MARY PARKER FOLLETT

The team developer realizes that at times the leadership "torch" must be passed on to others. This empowerment of others serves a dual purpose; it helps them hone their own team-building skills and it brings a fresh approach, perhaps even a special expertise, to the group's efforts.

M A R L E N E   C A R O S E L L I

Leaders are like gardeners. . . . As leaders we are not only responsible for harvesting our own success but for cultivating the success of the next generation.

S U S A N   C O L L I N S

The highest type of leadership is serving other people in such a way that they lead themselves, that they develop spiritually. An authentic leader helps others increase their own independence, and he does not actually give direction or assert authority.

S Y L V I A   B U S H E L L

In a future world where workers expect greater self-fulfillment from their work and organizations are faced with a rapidly changing social and economic environment, we will need women and men who, as leaders, can nurture the human potential of their followers.

TRUDY HELLER

A powerful woman leader empowers others and provides a safe environment for them to express their opinions.

MARILYN MANNING AND PATRICIA HADDOCK

To empower others is ultimately to empower oneself.

MARY ELIZABETH SCHLAYER

Our success multiplies each time we lead someone else to success.

SUSAN COLLINS

Once you feel that power, the joy, and the results that come from freeing yourself up, then, if you're any kind of human being, and especially if you're a leader, you'll want other people to have that feeling. A leader has to find ways to help people have that feeling without giving up who he is.

SANDY LINVER

The best leaders try to train their followers themselves to become leaders. . . . They wish to be leaders of leaders.

MARY PARKER FOLLETT

Leadership, in a very real sense, is helping others develop their leadership.

SYLVIA BUSHELL

Effective leaders let people discover things for themselves.

JEAN ILLSLEY CLARKE

A true leader is constantly providing tools that enable independence. The timing and the selection of the presented tools is the exercise of leadership or wisdom.

SYLVIA BUSHELL

People are capable of more than their organizational positions ever give them the tools or the time or the opportunity to demonstrate.

ROSABETH MOSS KANTER

A good manager spends a lot of time teaching. It's very hard to practice this because it doesn't seem immediately productive. It usually takes less time to do something yourself than to explain how to do it to someone else. But then you may have to do it a thousand times instead of explaining it only once.

DIANE TRACY

The point of educating instead of blaming seems to me very important. For nothing stultifies one more than being blamed. Moreover, if the question is, who is to blame?, perhaps each will want to place the blame on someone else, or on the other hand, someone may try to shield his fellow-worker. In either case the attempt is to hide the error and if this is done the error cannot be corrected.

MARY PARKER FOLLETT

Never hesitate to show your own staff that you need help. They need to be reminded how important they are to the process. . . . People sometimes forget how much interdependence there really is in a successful business. Learn the art of asking for help to empower and motivate others, and you will have learned a very powerful management strategy.

GEORGETTE MOSBACHER

No leader can be too far ahead of his followers.

ELEANOR ROOSEVELT

One of the most important lessons of the workplace is knowing when to ask for help. If I make a mistake, I know the best thing to do is notify people who can help solve it.

VALERIE WOHLLEBER

As leaders, we live under a microscope. Nothing we say or do escapes the scrutiny and examination of our followers.

SHEILA MURRAY BETHEL

Your attitude as a leader will set the pace and tone for your employees. People tend to mirror each other, and employees especially tend to mirror their managers.

MARILYN MANNING AND PATRICIA HADDOCK

The speed of the leader is the speed of the gang.

MARY KAY ASH

Employees are not your family, or even your friends. Don't drag personal emotions or relationships into the business situation.

JANE WESMAN

Motivation begins with the job interview. If you hire the wrong person, you will never be able to motivate him or her, no matter how hard you try.

JANE WESMAN

I make it a *point* to hire people who know more than I do, then I try to get the most out of them. The real value of a manager at any level comes in bringing the best out of everybody on the team.

GRACE PASTIAK

Y ou run a major risk when you assume that you alone have all the answers: You don't, and that's okay. You don't have to be afraid to admit there are certain things you either don't like to do or aren't any good at. You reach a goal by covering all your bases, and you cover all your bases by hiring good people.

GEORGETTE MOSBACHER

Hiring employees is often a bigger gamble than putting all your money on one number in Las Vegas. At least there, you know what you are betting on. When you hire an employee, all you know is what you think you're betting on, but in reality, you won't know the outcome for a few weeks or months. . . . Usually, the higher the status of your employees, the longer it takes to evaluate their worth. . . . You will know after a few days if a secretary will work out, but for a manager, this may take months.

MARCILLE GRAY WILLIAMS

Always hire people who are better than you. Hiring dummies is shortsighted. You can't move up the ladder until everyone is comfortable with your replacement.

LOIS WYSE

People want to do a good job. They do not make mistakes because they think it's fun, or because they want to spite you or make you lose money.

JANE WESMAN

Just as managers must allow themselves to fail, so should they allow—even encourage—their subordinates to do so. Not to say that repeated mistakes are acceptable, but if your employees fear failure, they will never takes risks, never learn from their mistakes, and never do their best work.

CONNIE GLASER AND
BARBARA STEINBERG SMALLEY

You take people as far as they will go, not as far as you would like them to go.

JEANNETTE RANKIN

One can present people with opportunities. One cannot make them equal to them.

ROSAMOND LEHMANN

When we're impatient with beginners around us, we would do well to sign up for a class in scuba diving, ballroom dancing or anything else totally brand-new for us.

SUSAN COLLINS

"Rules for Stifling Innovation": 1. Regard any new idea from below with suspicion—because it's new, and because it's from below. 2. Insist that people who need your approval to act first go through several other levels of management to get their signatures. 3. Ask departments or individuals to challenge and criticize each other's proposals. (That saves you the job of deciding; you just pick the survivor.) . . . 10. And above all, never forget that you, the higher-ups, already know everything important about this business.

ROSABETH MOSS KANTER

Wise leaders know that if an individual doesn't count, the institution doesn't count for much either. Put mathematically, if the individual is a zero, together a lot of zeros add up to a whole lot of nothing.

DIANE DREHER

We often tend to think that the executive wishes to maintain standards, wishes to reach a certain quality of production, and that the worker has to be goaded in some way to do this. Again and again we forget that the worker is often, usually I think, equally interested, that his greatest pleasure in his work comes from the satisfaction of worthwhile accomplishment, of having done the best of which he was capable.

MARY PARKER FOLLETT

Treat others as though you work for them even though they work for you.

EVELYN DUNN

Leaders value other people's worth and opinions and take the time to let them know they are important. It doesn't take very much time to pay someone a compliment. The average is six seconds.

CONNIE PODESTA AND JEAN GATZ

To hear how special and wonderful we are is endlessly enthralling.

GAIL SHEEHY

What you praise you increase.

CATHERINE PONDER

A common saying in business is: The customer is always right. In the case of management, it should be: Your staff is always right . . . at least as far as the public is concerned. . . . You will have to sweat sometimes in order to have staff members worth any salt, and part of that sweat will result from defending them from others . . . sometimes others with power.

LAURIE BETH JONES

Patting the back knocks a chip off the shoulder.

MURIEL SOLOMON

Studies show that children laugh an average of four hundred times a day. In contrast, adults laugh an average of fifteen times a day. Pathetic, isn't it? As a manager, *you* can help boost these statistics by lightening up yourself and encouraging those who work for you to work hard at getting more "smileage" out of life.

CONNIE GLASER AND
BARBARA STEINBERG SMALLEY

Sandwich every bit of criticism between two heavy layers of praise.

MARY KAY ASH

Praise keeps productivity and quality high. This works especially with those who do routine jobs over a long period of time. We all appreciate recognition. No one can ever get too much approval.

PRISCILLA ELFREY

There are two things that people want more than sex and money—recognition and praise.

MARY KAY ASH

If you think a complimentary thought about someone, don't just think it. Dare to compliment people and pass on compliments to them from others.

CATHERINE PONDER

Whenever I meet someone, I try to imagine him wearing an invisible sign that says: MAKE ME FEEL IMPORTANT! I respond to this sign immediately, and it works wonders. . . . I think it's essential that every manager remember that invisible sign: MAKE ME FEEL IMPORTANT!

MARY KAY ASH

The most notable fact that culture imprints on women is the sense of our limits. The most important thing one woman can do for another is to illuminate and expand her sense of actual possibilities.

A D R I E N N E   R I C H

The leader has to strike a balance between, on the one hand, acknowledging success and helping people to feel good about what they've accomplished, and, on the other, creating or maintaining the discomfort necessary to keep people moving. . . . The art of effective leadership lies in steering between complacency and discouragement.

S A N D Y   L I N V E R

I believe every person has the ability to achieve something important, and with that in mind I regard everyone as special. A manager should feel this way about people, but it's an attitude that can't be faked. You've got to be honestly convinced that every human being is important.

MARY KAY ASH

When you're feeling smug because you've heard no complaints, that's the time to worry.

MURIEL SOLOMON

I am convinced that any feeling of exaltation because we have people under us should be conquered, for I am sure that if we enjoy being over people, there will be something in our manner which will make them dislike being under us.

MARY PARKER FOLLETT

Micromanaging erodes people's confidence, making them overly dependent on their leaders. Well-meaning leaders inadvertently sabotage their teams by rushing to the rescue and offering too much help. A leader needs to balance assistance with *wu wei*, backing off long enough to let people learn from their mistakes and develop competence.

D I A N E   D R E H E R

Many people think that controlling people is what management is about. Leaders should have no time to control people. You're busy enough thinking, planning, discussing, interacting, suggesting, bargaining, negotiating, and checking. Controlling others is not the main event. It is less important than establishing objectives on which those who depend on you for a salary can focus.

P R I S C I L L A   E L F R E Y

If I believe that I am in control because you have accepted my ideas, then I am deluding myself. There is a lot of self-delusion in management. You can control people only when you intimidate them and remain there to keep up the pressure.

PRISCILLA ELFREY

The rule of good management is that when things go wrong in your area it's your fault; when things go right it's because of the people who report to you.

DIANE TRACY

If you're good to your staff when things are going well, they'll rally when times go bad.

MARY KAY ASH

Delegation

Wise leaders learn early in their careers to maximize their influence on any given project by inviting the participation of talented subordinates. The art of leadership, in fact, has been described by some corporate leaders as the process of turning one's work over to others.

DAYLE M. SMITH

I don't keep a dog and bark myself.

ELIZABETH I

55

By delegating both the symbols and realities of power to subordinates, the manager has more time for the real work of leadership: establishing and setting goals, evaluating progress.

PRISCILLA ELFREY

Delegation of authority requires a tremendous amount of trust. Perhaps that is why there are so many confused employees, because there are so many fearful people at the top. If leaders operate out of fear, they cannot delegate. A leader who does not delegate will end up with a group of "yes" people who will ultimately lead to his or her demise.

LAURIE BETH JONES

Learning to delegate appropriate work to the appropriate person is a necessary skill that will enable you to work smarter, faster, and better.

CONNIE PODESTA AND JEAN GATZ

When you delegate, your team members learn to think like leaders and the commitment and energy of the team can increase dramatically.

MARILYN MANNING
AND PATRICIA HADDOCK

Delegation is necessary and risky. People will do things differently. Your instructions will probably be misunderstood. What you say is likely to be different from what they hear.

PRISCILLA ELFREY

My philosophy is that you can't do anything yourself. Your people have to do it.

BETH PRITCHARD

Women have made their reputation within the company on their task performance, diligence, and concrete accomplishments. They face a turnaround in their priorities when they move from worker to manager. Their task, as manager, is to stop doing so much of the work. Paradoxically, the strengths that elevated a woman to manager are transformed into shortcomings within that position. Women who have always done more than their share of the work must learn to relinquish the substance of tasks to their subordinates.

SUE JOAN MENDELSON FREEMAN

If someone was to tally the number of human hours wasted in business by people trying to accomplish objectives without being given the authority to do so, we would all be appalled.

LAURIE BETH JONES

Decision-Making

Decision-making is one of the most important components for an executive. You have to say either yes or no, even though a yes or no may be wrong at the time. You can't leave people in a vacuum. Be definitive.

HELEN MAYER

It's better to be boldly decisive and risk being wrong than to agonize at length and be right too late.

MARILYN MOATS KENNEDY

I once heard a business lecturer say that if an executive makes just 50 percent of her decisions correctly, she can be successful. The key is to make them.

MARCILLE GRAY WILLIAMS

A decision-maker must be willing to accept her limits, to recognize that she, like other mortals, will at times make poor and inappropriate decisions. Yet an effective leader does not lament, "How dumb I was to make that decision!" Instead, she says, "Well, I made the best decision I could *at that time*"—and believes that statement.

LOIS BORLAND HART

All decisions are made on insufficient evidence.

RITA MAE BROWN

All choices are gambles. An effective leader is one who minimizes the risks without being paralyzed by the fear of gambling. An effective leader knows when to admit to being wrong and when to cut the losses. In short, an effective leader admits to being human without using that as an excuse for being indecisive.

MADELINE MARIE DANIELS

No matter how much information you collect, no decision comes with guarantees.

MADELINE MARIE DANIELS

Indecision is fatal. It is better to make a wrong decision than to build up a habit of indecision.

MARIE BEYNON RAY

If we wait until we are 100 percent sure that we are making the Right rather than the Wrong decision, we can be 100 percent sure of only one thing—we will never make any decision at all. To be decisive and proactive, we often need to act *long before* we're convinced we're doing the right thing. Effective managers are labeled effective, not necessarily because of the number of correct decisions they make, but because they can make decisions, period.

ARLEEN LaBELLA AND DOLORES LEACH

When anxiety, fear, uncertainty, and ambivalence prevail, leaders must *act*. When anxiety levels are high, not deciding and/or not acting increases people's sense of uncertainty and decreases people's confidence in the leader.

JUDITH M. BARDWICK

It has been said that there are three kinds of people: those who make things happen, those who watch things happen, and those who wonder what happened. Because the planning function is essential to effective organizational leadership, leaders cannot watch or wonder; they must do and plan.

LOIS BORLAND HART

There is no such thing as a free ticket; every decision has both opportunity and cost.

PRISCILLA ELFREY

Decision is a sharp knife that cuts clean and straight. Indecision is a dull one that hacks and tears and leaves ragged edges behind.

JAN MCKEITHEN

Another idea that is changing is that the leader must be one who can make quick decisions. The leader today is often one who thinks out his decisions very slowly.

MARY PARKER FOLLETT

The most important thing a leader must keep in mind during the decision-making process is the distinction between compliance (getting people to act) and commitment (getting people to want to act). The command approach gets people to act while the consultative or delegative approach can inspire them to want to act.

MARY GAIL BIEBEL

In preparing for planning responsibilities, it is extremely important to be clear on your own philosophy—your beliefs and attitudes about yourself and others, your view of human nature, and your conceptions of the role of institutions in society. . . . Each decision a leader makes reflects either a personal or organizational philosophy.

LOIS BORLAND HART

The mind gives us thousands of ways to say no, but there's only one way to say yes, and that's from the heart.

SUZE ORMAN

The most painful moral struggles are not those between good and evil, but between the good and the lesser good.

BARBARA GRIZZUTI HARRISON

Standing in the middle of the road is very dangerous; you get knocked down by traffic from both sides.

MARGARET THATCHER

One advantage of consensus is that you can get a broader participation. But you have to know when the moment has been reached to say, well, OK, now I have to assume my responsibility.

MARIA LIBERIA-PETERS

Do not wait for ideal circumstances; they will never come.

JANET ERSKINE STUART

It is always the sign of the second-rate man when the decision merely meets the present situation. It is the left-over in a decision which gives it its greatest value. It is the carry-over in the decision which helps develop the situation in the way we wish it to be developed.

MARY PARKER FOLLETT

To think too long about doing a thing often becomes its undoing.

EVA YOUNG

If you have to swallow a toad, don't stare at it too long.

CONNIE HILLIARD

When a decision has been made and the die is cast, then murder the alternatives.

MRS. EMORY S. ADAMS, JR.

A peacefulness follows any decision, even the wrong one.

RITA MAE BROWN

Change

Change is the constant, the signal for rebirth, the egg of the phoenix.

CHRISTINA BALDWIN

Learning how to respond to and master the process of change—and even to excel at it—is a critical leadership skill for the twenty-first century. Constant, rapid change will be a fact of life for all of us.

JENNIFER JAMES

Developing the abilities and attitudes to deal adequately with change—particularly those that appear to be negative—should be our highest priority.

PRISCILLA ELFREY

Fluidity and discontinuity are central to the reality in which we live.

MARY CATHERINE BATESON

The things we fear most in organizations—fluctuations, disturbances, imbalances—need not be signs of an impending disorder that will destroy us. Instead, fluctuations are the primary source of creativity.

MARGARET J. WHEATLEY

Individuals learn faster than institutions and it is always the dinosaur's brain that is the last to get the new messages!

HAZEL HENDERSON

Nostalgia is also a trait of [some] organizations. . . . Their bonding power often exceeds loyalty to family or country because they create intimacy through shared ideals and beliefs, ceremonies, stories, and legends, and depend on it for their survival. The message is clear: Don't question what we're doing. Just appreciate how long we've been doing it.

JENNIFER JAMES

Things good in themselves . . . perfectly valid in the integrity of their origins, become fetters if they cannot alter.

FREYA STARK

Everyone, including those who proposed or implemented the change, experiences "loss." This may be manifested as disorientation, loss of identity, loss of security, uncertainty, or disenchantment. They may feel ambivalence about the future as they move from what was "known" and comfortable, to what is "unknown" and therefore less comfortable.

DELORESE AMBROSE

Leaders know that trust is a competitive advantage in a world of adversarial competition. Basically, trust is a matter of predictability. People trust others when they are told that something will happen and it does. Major change, therefore, always threatens trust and thus, ultimately, confidence in leadership.

JUDITH M. BARDWICK

It's unbelievable the primitive feelings that are aroused by rapid change.

SHEILA BALLANTYNE

Yesterday people were permitted to change things. They will be permitted to advocate changing them tomorrow. It is only dangerous to think of changing anything today.

ELIZABETH HAWES

All birth is unwilling.

PEARL S. BUCK

There is no sin punished more implacably by nature than the sin of resistance to change.

ANNE MORROW LINDBERGH

As leaders we are most effective at promoting change when we are able to draw on both our personal power (the lessons learned from resolving life struggles) and organizational power (our position, expertise, and knowledge).

DELORESE AMBROSE

When you're stuck in a spiral, to change all aspects of the spin you need only to change one thing.

CHRISTINA BALDWIN

If you wish to make changes in your office and your job, remember that you are the most important variable. You have more control over yourself than you will ever have over any external variable. And since people and events are interrelated, any change in you will provoke corresponding changes in the environment.

MADELINE MARIE DANIELS

You have control over three things—*what you think*, *what you say* and *how you behave*. To make a change in your life, you must recognize that these gifts are the most powerful tools you possess in shaping the form of your life.

SONYA FRIEDMAN

Change provides us with experiences that we convert to personal power.

BYLLYE AVERY

Change can be exhilarating, refreshing—a chance to meet challenges, a chance to clean house. It means excitement when it is considered normal, when people expect it routinely, like a daily visit from the mail carrier—known—bringing a set of new messages—unknown. Change brings opportunities when people have been planning for it, are ready for it, and have just the thing in mind to do when the new state comes into being.

ROSABETH MOSS KANTER

If you had to choose only two qualities to get you through times of change, the first should be a sense of self-worth and the second a sense of humor.

J E N N I F E R   J A M E S

So often I heard people paying blind obeisance to change—as though it had some virtue of its own. Change or we will die. Change or we will stagnate. Evergreens don't stagnate.

J U D I T H   R O S S N E R

You must not change one thing, one pebble, one grain of sand, until you know what good and evil will follow on that act.

U R S U L A   K .   L E   G U I N

The difference between transformation by accident and transformation by a system is like the difference between lightning and a lamp. Both give illumination, but one is dangerous and unreliable, while the other is relatively safe, directed, available.

MARILYN FERGUSON

Adaptable as human beings are and have to be, I sometimes sympathize with the chameleon who had a nervous breakdown on a patchwork quilt.

JOHN STEPHEN STRANGE

Conflict

That is the wearisome part of business—
there is no peace, no sense of certain, permanent
achievement, no stability. The unexpected, and usually
the awful, is forever happening.

ALICE FOOTE MACDOUGALL

Your first big trouble can be a bonanza
if you live through it. Get through the first trouble,
you'll probably make it through the next one.

RUTH GORDON

Every time you meet a situation, though you think at the time it is an impossibility and you go through the torture of the damned, once you have met it and lived through it, you find that forever after you are freer than you were before.

ELEANOR ROOSEVELT

Managers must be able to accept conflict as an inevitable part of organizational life. For just as the process of change is becoming a given throughout industry, so the conflicts that inevitably result from change are also becoming a way of life in most organizations. . . . Once conflict is seen as an inevitable by-product of change rather than as something either positive or negative, it is easier to approach, understand, and resolve effectively.

MARILYN LODEN

Unity, not uniformity, must be our aim. We attain unity only through variety. Differences must be integrated, not annihilated, nor absorbed.

MARY PARKER FOLLETT

What people often mean by getting rid of conflict is getting rid of diversity, and it is of the utmost importance that these should not be considered the same.

MARY PARKER FOLLETT

It does not so much matter what happens. It is what one does when it happens that really counts.

LAURA INGALLS WILDER

There are three ways of dealing with difference: domination, compromise, and integration. By domination only one side gets what it wants; by compromise neither side gets what it wants; by integration we find a way by which both sides may get what they wish.

MARY PARKER FOLLETT

When people are at loggerheads, sometimes they just need encouragement to keep going. I try to show people that I have every confidence in them—that can often help turn a situation around.

NANCY BADORE

The single most dangerous word to be spoken in business is "no." The second most dangerous word is "yes." It is possible to avoid saying either.

LOIS WYSE

You start by saying no to requests. Then if you have to go to yes, OK. But if you start with yes, you can't go to no.

MILDRED PERLMAN

Give in on small issues. In the long haul, you get more that way.

JANICE LAROUCHE AND REGINA RYAN

An apology is the superglue of life. It can repair just about anything.

LYNN JOHNSTON

A crisis is only a turning point.

ANNE LINDTHORST

To have a crisis, and act upon it, is one thing.
To dwell in perpetual crisis is another.

BARBARA GRIZZUTI HARRISON

Things that don't get better, get worse.

ELLEN SUE STERN

Empathy is the biggest negotiation tool.
I must try to understand where the other person's
coming from to make points for my side.

LEE DUCAT

Let the other side break it [the silence]. If there is silence, it's because you've reached an impasse, and generally the side that breaks the impasse either has to come up with a compromise or say something to reinitiate the discussion. And more often than not, it's a softening of their position.

SUSAN PRAVDA

When confronted by conflict and confusion, another practice is to take a deep breath, pause and ask: "Where is the gift in this?"

DIANE DREHER

Most of us work in places where a person who wants to block something has an easier route than a person who wants to accomplish something.

PRISCILLA ELFREY

Those who attack always do so with greater fervor than those who defend.

ELEANOR ROOSEVELT

When you get promoted, you may find yourself having to give assignments and criticism to people with whom you formerly had a very different relationship—quite equal and quite friendly. It can be a difficult predicament. Your friend or ex-peer may not take your requests seriously, or may not take you seriously. He or she may in every way resist the shift in rank and continue to treat you in the same old way. The company has promoted you—but your friends won't.

JANICE LAROUCHE AND REGINA RYAN

Accept it: You will be criticized this year.
Maybe even this week. Maybe even in an hour.

KAREN SALMANSOHN

Openly questioning the way the world
works and challenging the power of the powerful is
not an activity customarily rewarded.

DALE SPENDER

Disturbers are never popular—nobody
ever really loved an alarm clock in action, no matter
how grateful he may have been afterwards for its kind
services!

NELLIE L. McCLUNG

If you have any interest at all in moving into a position of power . . . it is absolutely necessary to manage the feeling of being unliked, unpopular and left out.

ARLEEN LABELLA AND DOLORES LEACH

It's important that people should know what you stand for. It's equally important that they know what you won't stand for.

MARY WALDRIP

Curiously enough, it is often the people who refuse to assume any responsibility who are apt to be the sharpest critics of those who do.

ELEANOR ROOSEVELT

When somebody says, "I hope you won't mind my telling you this," it's pretty certain that you will.

SYLVIA BREMER

Don't ever take advice from anyone who starts a sentence with, "You may not like me for this, but it's for your own good—" It never is.

LOIS WYSE

If you want a place in the sun, you've got to put up with a few blisters.

ABIGAIL VAN BUREN

I have spent many years of my life in opposition, and I rather like the role.

ELEANOR ROOSEVELT

One of the greatest values of controversy is its revealing nature. The real issues at stake come into the open and have the possibility of being reconciled.

MARY PARKER FOLLETT

Only the fittest will survive, and the fittest will be the ones who understand their office's politics.

JEAN HOLLANDS

Unlike lions and dogs, we are a dissenting animal. We need to dissent in the same way that we need to travel, to make money, to keep a record of our time on earth and in dream, and to leave a permanent mark. Dissension is a drive, like those drives.

CAROL BLY

Providence has hidden a charm in difficult undertakings, which is appreciated only by those who dare to grapple with them.

ANNE-SOPHIE SWETCHINE

When people keep telling you that you can't do a thing, you kind of like to try it.

MARGARET CHASE SMITH

Even when you think people are wrong, it is easy to tell when they are right. When they are right about something you are trying very hard to hide from others and yourself, you know they are right because you want to kill them.

C ANDICE B ERGEN

If you can keep your head when all about you are losing theirs, it's just possible you haven't grasped the situation.

J EAN K ERR

Risks

Leaders are willing to put themselves on the line. I don't believe you can play it safe and be a leader.

SANDY LINVER

Not all risktakers are leaders. Not everybody wants to be a leader. However, all leaders are risktakers because they create new ideas and visions and have to convince others to follow them.

DOROTHY W. CANTOR AND TONI BERNAY

Through the experiences I have had and the risks I have taken, I have gained courage and confidence. I didn't start with the courage and confidence. I started with the risk.

L A U R A   D A V I S

People who refuse to take risks live with a feeling of dread that is far more severe than what they would feel if they took the risks necessary to make them less helpless—only they don't know it!

S U S A N   J E F F E R S

Risk always brings its own rewards: the exhilaration of breaking through, of getting to the other side; the relief of a conflict healed; the clarity when a paradox dissolves. Whoever teaches us this is the agent of our liberation. Eventually we know deeply that the other side of every fear is freedom.

M A R I L Y N   F E R G U S O N

You have to be careful about being too careful.

BERYL PFIZER

Institutions which have too much security . . . tend to become bureaucratic. They add layers of people and layers of rules in order to assure the security of not making mistakes.

JUDITH M. BARDWICK

Risk! Risk anything! Care no more for the opinions of others, for those voices. Do the hardest thing on earth for you. Act for yourself. Face the truth.

KATHERINE MANSFIELD

Motivation is highest when the probability of success is 50 percent: We don't get involved if the task is too easy or too hard.

JUDITH M. BARDWICK

A ship in port is safe, but that's not what ships are built for.

GRACE MURRAY HOPPER

I would not creep along the coast, but steer
Out in mid-sea, by guidance of the stars.

GEORGE ELIOT

When people in organizations feel too secure, it's because there aren't any significant outcomes as a result of what they do. Whatever you do, nothing much different happens. This also means there are no important pay-offs if you risk by innovating. As there are no rewards for taking risks, then there's no sense of *push* in that institution's culture.

JUDITH M. BARDWICK

The difference between a calculated risk and rolling the dice can be expressed in one word: homework.

GEORGETTE MOSBACHER

We know that productivity suffers when uncertainty is high. But we've failed to realize the equally destructive effects of too little anxiety. People are not at their keenest when life is too safe. When people receive without having to achieve they are protected from failure. There's no punishment for not achieving. At first glance that may seem like a good thing, but it is not. By protecting people from risk, we destroy their self-esteem. We rob them of the opportunity to become strong, competent people.

JUDITH M. BARDWICK

Luck enters into every contingency. You are a fool if you forget it—and a greater fool if you count upon it.

PHYLLIS BOTTOME

The fullness of life is in the hazards of life.

EDITH HAMILTON

If you risk nothing, then you risk everything.

GEENA DAVIS

If you don't risk anything, you risk even *more*.

ERICA JONG

Sometimes I think we can tell how important it is to risk by how dangerous it would be to do so.

SONIA JOHNSON

If you're never scared or embarrassed or hurt, it means you never take any chances.

JULIA SOREL

All my life I have gone out on a limb, but I have turned the limb into a bridge, and there is cool, clear water flowing under.

HOLLY NEAR

All serious daring starts from within.

EUDORA WELTY

Visions and Dreams

The ablest administrators do not merely draw logical conclusions from the array of facts of the past which their expert assistants bring to them, they have a vision of the future.

MARY PARKER FOLLETT

Leaders shape our visions of the possible and direct our energies toward it.

MARCIA LYNN WHICKER

The leaders I admire have a clear vision of how things should be. They are able to communicate that vision so others can share in it, and then get others to work together as a unit, each contributing his or her best toward the achievement of that vision.

SARA E. MELÉNDEZ

Leaders are visionaries. They see the outcome. Leaders are communicators. They tell us what they're seeing. They hold the dream, letting us feel that it's possible. Our minds open up to what they show us could be. We dream with them. We get excited with them, drawing on all our abilities to create the future.

SUSAN COLLINS

As a good gardener prepares the soil, so a wise leader creates an environment that promotes community. . . . Community involves a common place, a common time, and a common purpose. Just getting people in the same place at the same time does not produce a team. Community requires a common vision.

DIANE DREHER

Leader and followers are both following the invisible leader—the common purpose. The best executives put this common purpose clearly before their group. While leadership depends on depth of conviction and the power coming therefrom, there must also be the ability to share that conviction with others, the ability to make purpose articulate. And then that common purpose becomes the leader.

MARY PARKER FOLLETT

Where another person sees problems, a leader sees possibilities. . . . Leaders must have the courage to follow their vision, to believe in the invisible, to work for something that's still only a possibility, while others often wring their hands in despair.

DIANE DREHER

The leader is the primary keeper and originator of the vision, but it's her responsibility to help others own it, too, not to impose it.

SANDY LINVER

The leader should have the spirit of adventure, but the spirit of adventure need not mean the temperament of the gambler. It should be the pioneer spirit which blazes new trails. The insight to see possible new paths, the courage to try them, the judgment to measure results—these are the qualifications of the leader.

MARY PARKER FOLLETT

Reach high, for stars lie hidden in your soul. Dream deep, for every dream precedes the goal.

PAMELA VAULL STARR

Whatever your mind can conceive and believe, it can achieve.

BARBARA A. ROBINSON

Far away there in the sunshine are my highest aspirations. I may not reach them, but I can look up and see their beauty, believe in them and try to follow where they lead.

LOUISA MAY ALCOTT

It is necessary that we dream now and then. No one ever achieved anything from the smallest to the greatest unless the dream was dreamed first.

LAURA INGALLS WILDER

The people who dream are very often the people who see, and dreaming and seeing precede doing.

MARGARET E. SANGSTER

As you enter positions of trust and power, dream a little before you think.

TONI MORRISON

Goals are dreams with deadlines.

DIANA SCHARF HUNT

Generally speaking, followers will not commit themselves for very long to a leader who is not also a pragmatist. As most of us have discovered, dreams are only powerful when we believe they can come true. Pipe dreams belong in the realm of fantasy; leaders' dreams belong in the realm of possibility.

MARLENE CAROSELLI

Passion

Leaders have passion and are willing to show it.

SANDY LINVER

Passion is the engagement of our soul with something beyond us, something that helps us put up with or fight against insurmountable odds, even at high risks, because it is all worth it.

JANET O. HAGBERG

People don't care how much you know until they know how much you care.

SHEILA MURRAY BETHEL

The difference between ordinary and extra-ordinary is that little "extra"!

ANONYMOUS

Enthusiasm is the divine particle in our composition: with it we are great, generous, and true; without it, we are little, false, and mean.

L.E. LANDON

No stair is steep to happy feet!

MARY F. ROBINSON

Enthusiasm is contagious. Be a carrier.

SUSAN RABIN

When you put yourself wholeheartedly into something, energy grows. It seems inexhaustible. If, on the other hand, you are divided and conflicted about what you are doing, you create anxiety. And the amount of physical and emotional energy consumed by anxiety is exorbitant.

HELEN DE ROSIS

You will do foolish things, but do them with enthusiasm.

COLETTE

A mediocre idea that generates enthusiasm will go further than a great idea that inspires no one.

MARY KAY ASH

A faint endeavor ends in a sure defeat.

HANNAH MORE

People with passion are incredibly inventive and tenacious individuals. They go way beyond the call of duty and frequently either work on their passion without pay or give more of themselves than their pay warrants.

JANET O. HAGBERG

Intuition

Intuition is the ability to tap into the reality behind circumstances and events.

SYLVIA BUSHELL

You can't solve many of today's problems by straight linear thinking. It takes leaps of faith to sense the connections that are not necessarily obvious.

MATINA HORNER

Trust your gut.

BARBARA WALTERS

Intuition is a combination of insight and imagination that was once attributed to spiritual communication. Mathematicians call it "fuzzy logic," drawing conclusions from vague or subjective input. The mind becomes aware without the direct intervention of reasoning. Once you can imagine something you can begin the process of creating it. Executives use intuition to make many product, investment, and hiring decisions, even if they deny it. Success in business may depend on an accurate gut.

JENNIFER JAMES

Sometimes I'll trust my gut more than my head. Logical information might lead me in one direction and my feelings in another. Whereas I would have followed my head ten years ago, now I'm as likely or more likely to go with my gut feeling. It's ironic— you'd think the opposite would be true as you move to the top but it's not.

DONNA SHALALA

There is always one true inner voice. Trust it.

GLORIA STEINEM

Successful executives and effective leaders are open to feedback; they use it to explore where they are both intellectually and emotionally, and how that relates to who they want to be and need to be in their world; but they don't let it shape who they are. They know that all the really important answers are inside themselves.

SANDY LINVER

Your intuition never sleeps. It fills your dreams as well as your waking hours with information from your unconscious and from the environment around you. As you learn to give it your conscious attention, you reach toward yet another powerful internal resource.

NINA BOYD KREBS

The most important things ever said to us are said by our inner selves.

ADELAIDE BRY

When one is working out a problem . . . life becomes duality. One's ego transacts the ordinary routine of things, as if the mind had an upper and lower story and the regular performance of the day's duties moved and motivated on the upper floor, while down below the all-absorbing problem toils silently, forcefully, toward its solution.

ALICE FOOTE MACDOUGALL

You must create the space in your life to enable your inner guide to share her wisdom, her creativity, her vision, her courage. Unleashed, she is the single most potent resource you have.

MARILYN O. SIFFORD

Confidence

Above everything else leadership is confidence in our inner resources.

SYLVIA BUSHELL

Self-trust, we know, is the first secret of success.

LADY WILDE

People who succeed speak well of themselves to themselves.

LAURIE BETH JONES

The appearance of well-being, status, power, and prestige creates well-being, status, power, and prestige.

PRISCILLA ELFREY

There is no philosophy that will help us to succeed if we doubt our ability to do so.

JOAN KENNEDY

I have to remember to tell the negative committee that meets in my head to sit down and shut up.

KATHY KENDALL

We're all capable of climbing so much higher than we usually permit ourselves to suppose.

OCTAVIA BUTLER

The ability to envision positive outcomes is the essence of leadership.

DELORESE AMBROSE

There is an automatic assumption that negative is realistic and positive is unrealistic.

SUSAN JEFFERS

Real guts are nothing more than developing your inner voice to the point where it is louder and stronger than the voice of your fear.

GEORGETTE MOSBACHER

You must do the thing you think you cannot do.

ELEANOR ROOSEVELT

Belief in oneself is a crucial quality of leadership, because "a house divided against itself cannot stand." A leader who fluctuates back and forth sends a very wavery signal. Like the soprano who can shatter glass by finding that high note and holding it, a leader who can hold that high note, without wavering, can shatter walls.

LAURIE BETH JONES

I don't think you can make a contribution until you've moved *beyond* wondering if you're good enough.

NANCY BADORE

Leaders lead because they convince others that they understand the issues better than anyone else. People follow them because they speak about solutions with persuasive conviction, because they act decisively, and because they project confidence when others are uncertain.

JUDITH M. BARDWICK

If you don't know what you want, you'll probably get what somebody else wants.

SUSAN COLLINS

I have met many *wanna-bes*. I distinguish the *wannas* from the *gonnas* because the WBs all think someone else is to blame for their problems. . . . By contrast, GBs say: "What? There's no door here? I'll build one."

K. CALLAN

If you think you can, you can. And if you think you can't, you're right.

MARY KAY ASH

The body language that expresses confidence and authority is the easy, open stance, accompanied by direct eye contact with the other person.

CHERYL REIMOLD

I've gone through life believing in the strength and competence of others; never in my own. Now, dazzled, I discovered that *my* capacities were real. It was like finding a fortune in the lining of an old coat.

JOAN MILLS

Confidence is a plant of slow growth.

ANNA LEONOWENS

No one can make you feel inferior without your consent.

ELEANOR ROOSEVELT

My parents . . . always told me I could do anything but never told me how long it would take.

RITA RUDNER

Persistence

Whenyou get in a tight place and everything goes against you till it seems as though you
could not hold on a minute longer, never give up then,
for that is just the time and the place the tide will turn.

HARRIET BEECHER STOWE

It is with many enterprises as with striking
fire; we do not meet with success except by reiterated
efforts, and often at the instant when we despaired
of success.

MADAME DE MAINTENON

Aim at a high mark and you'll hit it. No, not the first time, nor the second time. Maybe not the third. But keep on aiming and keep on shooting for only practice will make you perfect.

ANNIE OAKLEY

Good enough never is.

DEBRA FIELD

If you defy the system long enough you'll be rewarded. At first life takes revenge and reduces you to a sniveling mess. But keep sniveling, have the madness, the audacity, to do what interests you, forget about your person, and eventually life will say all right, we'll let you do it.

JO COUDERT

Few wishes come true by themselves.

JUNE SMITH

One person who wants something is a hundred times stronger than a hundred who want to be left alone.

BARBARA WARD

Getting a project started is like moving a ship. It takes a lot of energy to build up momentum.

SUSAN COLLINS

You can eat an elephant one bite at a time.

MARY KAY ASH

One of the first principles of perseverance is to know when to stop persevering.

CAROLYN WELLS

Experience

Experience may be hard but we claim its gifts because they are real, even though our feet bleed on its stones.

MARY PARKER FOLLETT

If we could sell our experiences for what they cost us, we'd all be millionaires.

ABIGAIL VAN BUREN

A road twice traveled is never as long.

ROSALIE GRAHAM

Experience has no text books nor proxies. She demands that her pupils answer to her roll-call personally.

MINNA THOMAS ANTRIM

Good judgment is the outcome of experience . . . and experience is the outcome of bad judgment.

VIVIEN FUCHS

A rattlesnake that doesn't bite teaches you nothing.

JESSAMYN WEST

Unless the knowledge gained from experience is reconditioned in each new situation, it is a rigid and a dangerous guide.

BLANCHE H. DOW

Success

To tend, unfailingly, unflinchingly, towards a goal, is the secret of success.

A N N A   P A V L O V A

The secret of success is concentration; wherever there has been a great life, or a great work, that has gone before. Taste everything a little, look at everything a little, but live for one thing.

R A L P H   I R O N

Only when your consciousness is totally focused on the moment you are in can you receive whatever gift, lesson, or delight that moment has to offer.

BARBARA DE ANGELIS

Luck is a matter of preparation meeting opportunity.

OPRAH WINFREY

I do not know anyone who has got to the top without hard work. That is the recipe. It will not always get you to the top, but it should get you pretty near.

MARGARET THATCHER

Luck is not chance—
It's Toil—
Fortune's expensive smile
Is earned.

EMILY DICKINSON

It isn't success after all, is it, if it isn't an
expression of your deepest energies?

MARILYN FRENCH

People I know who succeed don't mind
working. Those who are competent seem to like doing
things well—not stopping because they haven't accomplished what they wanted to on the first go-round.
They're willing to do it twenty times, if necessary.
There's an illusion that the good people can *easily* do
something, and it's not necessarily true. They're just
determined to do it right.

SYLVIA A. EARLE

The road to success is a zigzag, first pointing this way and then that. If we start with high intention, then magic and coincidence will guide us there despite our lack of knowledge about what lies ahead.

SUSAN COLLINS

This seems to be the law of progress in everything we do; it moves along a spiral rather than a perpendicular; we seem to be actually going out of the way, and yet it turns out that we were really moving upward all the time.

FRANCES E. WILLARD

Success is getting up one more time than you fall down.

JULIE BOWDEN

I never wanted success if it meant clawing my way over other bodies. I always knew that would make it pretty lonely once I got there.

BARBARA GROGAN

I personally measure success in terms of the contributions an individual makes to her or his fellow human beings.

MARGARET MEAD

Success is completion. Success is being able to complete what we set out to do—each individual action, each specific step, each desired experience whether a big project or a very small errand.

SUSAN COLLINS

The need for challenge, the need to burst through the constrictions of tasks and situations already seen and mastered, can affect anyone, even those enjoying the greatest gains from success.

JUDITH M. BARDWICK

Achievement brings with it its own anticlimax.

AGATHA CHRISTIE

You always feel you are not deserving. People who are successful at what they do know what kind of work goes with it, so they are surprised at the praise.

VIRGINIA HAMILTON

Getting what you go after is success; but liking it while you are getting it is happiness.

BERTHA DAMON

Women on the way up generally fail to win popularity contests. The only compensation is that once you're there you will become very well liked.

LOIS WYSE

Success can make you go one of two ways. It can make you a prima donna, or it can smooth the edges, take away the insecurities, let the nice things come out.

BARBARA WALTERS

For you to be successful, sacrifices must be made. It's better that they are made by others but failing that, you'll have to make them yourself.

RITA MAE BROWN

Failure

The sheer rebelliousness in giving ourselves permission to fail frees a childlike awareness and clarity. . . . When we give ourselves permission to fail, we at the same time give ourselves permission to excel.

ELOISE RISTAD

If you haven't made any mistakes lately, you must be doing something wrong.

SUSAN JEFFERS

Failure is just another way to learn how to do something right.

MARIAN WRIGHT EDELMAN

A leader knows the difference between failure and learning.

MARILYN MANNING
AND PATRICIA HADDOCK

Coming to terms with failure is critical for managers, because otherwise you fear it and end up making safe decisions, which can stymie your career.

CONNIE GLASER AND
BARBARA STEINBERG SMALLEY

A series of failures may culminate in the best possible result.

GISELA M.A. RICHTER

People fail forward to success.

MARY KAY ASH

In a total work, the failures have their not unimportant place.

MAY SARTON

Thank goodness all flops aren't failures.

LILLIAN VERNON

If you have made mistakes, even serious ones, there is always another chance for you. What we call failure is not the falling down, but the staying down.

MARY PICKFORD

Mistakes are a fact of life.
It is the response to error that counts.

NIKKI GIOVANNI

Being defeated is often a temporary condition. Giving up is what makes it permanent.

MARILYN VOS SAVANT

There's nothing final about a mistake, except its being taken as final.

PHYLLIS BOTTOME

Some of the biggest failures I ever had were successes.

PEARL BAILEY

We may encounter many defeats but we must not be defeated.

MAYA ANGELOU

No one can become a winner without losing many, many times.

MARIE LINDQUIST

Just because you *made* a mistake doesn't mean you *are* a mistake.

GEORGETTE MOSBACHER

Our greatest weaknesses are always the flip side of our greatest strengths.

JUDITH SILLS

Sometimes what you want to do *has* to fail so you won't.

MARGUERITTE HARMON BRO

Do not think of today's failures, but of the success that may come tomorrow. You have set yourselves a difficult task, but you will succeed if you persevere; and you will find a joy in overcoming obstacles. Remember, no effort that we make to attain something beautiful is ever lost.

HELEN KELLER

What separates the winners from the losers is that winners are able to handle problems and crises that they never *imagined* would occur. You hit the floor, but what counts is how fast you can get up and regroup. Failure is simply part of the equation.

GEORGEITE MOSBACHER

It takes as much courage to have tried and failed as it does to have tried and succeeded.

ANNE MORROW LINDBERGH

You may be disappointed if you fail, but you are doomed if you don't try.

BEVERLY SILLS

Failure may be just a step toward your eventual goal.

GEORGETTE MOSBACHER

It's usually failure, disappointment, and frustration that motivate people to reexamine that which they've taken for granted. It's rare to find big change without significant bad news. It's only when the old ways of doing things are clearly not working that the path is cleared for new ways to be introduced. After all, if the old ways continue to generate success, it's immensely difficult to argue successfully for change. In that sense, the pain of failure creates the largest opportunities for progress.

JUDITH M. BARDWICK

I simply don't believe in failure. In itself, it doesn't exist. We create it. We make ourselves fail.

ALICE FOOTE MACDOUGALL

Failure?
I'm not ashamed to tell it,
I never learned to spell it.
Not Failure.

MAYA ANGELOU

The trick to managing failures, crises, and setbacks is not to avoid them, but to face them head-on, learn from them, and, when possible, make them work *for* you.

CONNIE GLASER AND
BARBARA STEINBERG SMALLEY

Swallowing your pride isn't lethal. It might upset your stomach for a few minutes, but the ultimate result may be the life of your dreams. And that's a result that's worth every rejection you encounter.

GEORGETTE MOSBACHER

Your worst humiliation is only someone else's momentary entertainment.

KAREN CROCKETT

Three failures denote uncommon strength. A weakling has not enough grit to fail thrice.

MINNA THOMAS ANTRIM

It is nothing to succeed if one has not taken great trouble, and it is nothing to fail if one has done the best one could.

NADIA BOULANGER

Typically, our love for our leaders is one-sided: their successes become our own, while their failures are theirs alone.

MARCIA LYNN WHICKER

Don't panic—at least not in front of others.

CONNIE GLASER AND
BARBARA STEINBERG SMALLEY

If at first you don't succeed, destroy all evidence that you tried.

SUSAN OHANIAN

Success and failure are both greatly overrated but failure gives you a whole lot more to talk about.

HILDEGARD KNEF

Work

Work itself is the reward. If I choose challenging work it will pay me back with interest. At least I'll be interested even if nobody else is. And this attempt for excellence is what sustains the most well lived and satisfying, successful lives.

MERYL STREEP

Work . . . has always been my favorite form of recreation.

ANNA HOWARD SHAW

149

Work is creativity accompanied by the comforting realization that one is bringing forth something really good and necessary, with the conviction that a sudden, arbitrary cessation would cause a sensitive void, produce a loss.

JENNY HEYNRICHS

To love what you do and feel that it matters—how could anything be more fun?

KATHARINE GRAHAM

I went back to being an amateur, in the sense of somebody who loves what she is doing. If a professional loses the love of work, routine sets in, and that's the death of work and of life.

ADE BETHUNE

To find joy in work is to discover the fountain of youth.

P E A R L   S .   B U C K

The ability to take pride in your own work is one of the hallmarks of sanity. Take away the ability to both work and be proud of it and you can drive anyone insane.

N I K K I   G I O V A N N I

When you're following your energy and doing what you want all the time, the distinction between work and play dissolves.

S H A K T I   G A W A I N

Do what you love, the money will follow.

M A R S H A   S I N E T A R

People are not the best because they work hard. They work hard because they are the best.

BETTE MIDLER

The harder you work the luckier you get.

SONYA FRIEDMAN

The only thing that ever sat its way to success was a hen.

SARAH BROWN

You can have unbelievable intelligence, you can have connections, you can have opportunities fall out of the sky. But in the end, hard work is the true, enduring characteristic of successful people.

MARSHA EVANS

It's not hard work that wears you out, but the repression of your true personality, and I've found a way of working that does not demand that.

FRANCES HESSELBEIN

I believe in hard work. It keeps the wrinkles out of the mind and the spirit.

HELENA RUBINSTEIN

Workaholics are energized rather than enervated by their work—their energy paradoxically expands as it is expended.

MARILYN MACHLOWITZ

It is not hard work which is dreary; it is superficial work.

EDITH HAMILTON

No job is a good job if it isn't good for you.

BARBARA DE ANGELIS

Work is a world apart from jobs. Work is the way you occupy your mind and hand and eye and whole body when they're informed by your imagination and wit, by your keenest perceptions, by your most profound reflections on everything you've read and seen and heard and been part of. You may or may not be paid to do your work.

ALICE KOLLER

Ideas

Ideas are power because ideas are money. Good ideas are hard to come by. They are rare. They are valuable.

JANE TRAHEY

The only people in the whole world who can change things are those who can sell ideas.

LOIS WYSE

After years of telling corporate citizens to "trust the system," many companies must relearn instead to trust their people—and encourage their people to use neglected creative capacities in order to tap the most potent economic stimulus of all: *idea power*.

ROSABETH MOSS KANTER

Ideas move rapidly when their time comes.

CAROLYN HEILBRUN

If you have one good idea, people will lend you twenty.

MARIE VON EBNER-ESCHENBACH

I had never been as resigned to ready-made ideas as I was to ready-made clothes, perhaps because, although I couldn't sew, I could think.

JANE RULE

At first people refuse to believe that a strange new thing can be done, then they begin to hope it can be done, then they see it can be done— then it is done and all the world wonders why it was not done centuries ago.

FRANCES HODGSON BURNETT

People who think in absolutes usually don't listen to anyone but themselves. They resist new ideas and try to preserve the status quo. . . . People who think they know usually stopped thinking long ago.

JENNIFER JAMES

General notions are generally wrong.

LADY MARY WORTLEY MONTAGU

Innovators are inevitably controversial.

EVA LE GALLIENNE

There are no new ideas. There are only new ways of making them felt.

AUDRE LORDE

There are no original ideas. There are only original people.

BARBARA GRIZZUTI HARRISON

True originality consists not in a new manner but in a new vision.

EDITH WHARTON

Beware of people carrying ideas. Beware of ideas carrying people.

BARBARA GRIZZUTI HARRISON

Communication

While leadership depends on depth of conviction and the power coming therefrom, there must also be the ability to share that conviction with others.

MARY PARKER FOLLETT

It seems the one thing that people are communicating about most these days is the need for better communication.

CONNIE PODESTA AND JEAN GATZ

Communication is the essential life blood of organizational life.

ANN HARRIMAN

Effective communication is the cement that binds an organization together. It is the foundation upon which successful teamwork and good customer relationships are built. It is no accident that employees who can communicate effectively and assertively soon find themselves in leadership roles.

CONNIE PODESTA AND JEAN GATZ

Leaders identify, articulate, and summarize concepts that motivate others. Most important, they boil concepts down to an understandable idea.

LAURIE BETH JONES

You simply cannot communicate enough. Experts say that you have to tell the average adult something six times before it is internalized. The challenge becomes communicating a message in such a creative way that it only has to be told once!

BARBARA A. GLANZ

It is possible to exchange "facts" without increasing the common area of understanding or creating unity. In this case there is only the simplest raw data being transferred. If the data is not meaningful as it is, then we need to communicate information. Information is the interpretation of data.

SYLVIA BUSHELL

Effective leaders don't hoard information and ideas because they know that knowledge is only power when it's shared with people who can implement the vision which that knowledge represents.

CONNIE PODESTA AND JEAN GATZ

The motive behind communication is to create unity between ourselves and others. Mostly we feel separate from others. Good communication makes us feel as if we are unified with others. This is the result of mutually beneficial interpretations of ideas and viewpoints.

SYLVIA BUSHELL

Anything you can do to creatively jazz up the memos and communications you send will result in more people actually reading them.

BARBARA A. GLANZ

If the mood is overly anxious, then anxiety must be reduced by lowering uncertainty. Very simply, uncertainty is reduced when people are told what's going on and what will happen to them. In the vacuum of no news, people imagine the worst. Since disappointment is much easier to handle than anxiety, then, good news or bad, honesty is honestly the best policy.

JUDITH M. BARDWICK

Give employees small bits of information about the business that they may not know. Then not only will they feel more pride in the organization as a whole and better understand their role in the overall process, but they can also help to educate your customers.

BARBARA A. GLANZ

To maintain trust, leadership must be consistent. Credibility is lost when there are big discrepancies between what leaders say and what they do. . . . Increasing credibility requires openness. Hidden agendas will destroy trust.

JUDITH M. BARDWICK

Organizations benefit when they require that managers always consider honesty an alternative. Sometimes the whole truth is inappropriate. You must distinguish between truth-telling and telling everything.

PRISCILLA ELFREY

When you tell the truth you increase people's sense of trust even if the news is bad. When anxiety is high and there's no real information, rumors multiply. And if people discover they've been lied to, rumors multiply even faster. Once the rumors start, they have a life cycle of their own. It becomes harder and harder to kill them.

JUDITH M. BARDWICK

The importance of discretion increases with closeness to the top of a hierarchical organization.

ROSABETH MOSS KANTER

Repeat nothing—absolutely nothing—that is told you in confidence. There is no such thing as telling just one person.

LOIS WYSE

If you can't say it to everybody, don't say it to anybody. There are people who will use what you have to say to undermine you or ingratiate themselves with someone else.

JANICE LAROUCHE AND REGINA RYAN

The office grapevine is 75% to 95% accurate and provides managers and staff with better information than formal communications, according to a recent study. Rather than ignore or try to repress the grapevine, it's crucial for executives to tune into it.

CAROL HYMOWITZ

Listening, not imitation, may be the sincerest form of flattery.

JOYCE BROTHERS

To feel as well as hear what someone says requires whole attention.

SYLVIA ASHTON-WARNER

Some of the most successful people managers are also the best listeners.

MARY KAY ASH

If you stand up to address a seated person, you gain height and a certain amount of temporary power. But if you face the person directly, on his level (whether sitting or standing), you are more likely to establish communication.

CHERYL REIMOLD

Why is it that when anything goes without saying, it never does?

MARCELENE COX

I know that after all is said and done, more is said than done.

RITA MAE BROWN

The less you talk, the more you're listened to.

ABIGAIL VAN BUREN

If you can't add to the discussion, don't subtract by talking.

LOIS WYSE

 Y ou can phrase something positively and
inspire people to do their best, or negatively and make
them feel worried, uncertain, and self-conscious. You
can talk at a fast pace and people will get nervous, feel
afraid to bring up extraneous thoughts. But those are
the very thoughts that might be most important! They
might represent that person's best thinking. If you're
rushed, you're simply not going to get at that extra
level of thinking.

F R A N C E S   H E S S E L B F I N

 S ay what you will in two
Words and get through.
Long, frilly
Palaver is silly.

M A R I E - F R A N Ç O I S E - C A T H E R I N E   D E   B E A U V E A U

It makes a great difference to a speaker whether he has something to say, or has to say something.

NELLIE L. MCCLUNG

The best impromptu speeches are the ones written well in advance.

RUTH GORDON

A speech does not need to be eternal to be immortal.

MURIEL HUMPHREY

Committees and Meetings

The length of a meeting rises with the number of people present and the productiveness of a meeting falls with the square of the number of people present.

EILEEN SHANAHAN

Committee meetings are always held at inconvenient times and usually take place in dark, dusty rooms the temperatures of which are unsuited to the human body.

VIRGINIA GRAHAM

If enough meetings are held, the meetings become more important than the problem.

SUSAN OHANIAN

The more committees you belong to, the less of ordinary life you will understand. When your daily round becomes nothing more than a daily round of committees you might as well be dead.

STELLA BENSON

Meetings . . . are rather like cocktail parties. You don't want to go, but you're cross not to be asked.

JILLY COOPER

A committee, of course, exists for the purpose of damping enthusiasms.

STELLA BENSON

The most likely place to have your idea-pocket picked is at a meeting. . . . Here an idea becomes public property the moment it hits the air waves.

JANE TRAHEY

Most people are not for or against anything; the first object of getting people together is to make them respond somehow, to overcome inertia. To disagree, as well as to agree, with people brings you closer to them.

MARY PARKER FOLLETT

Any committee is only as good as the most knowledgeable, determined and vigorous person on it. There must be somebody who provides the flame.

LADY BIRD JOHNSON

Keep track of who has not spoken. . . . It's also important to notice when people do speak out but are not heard. Effective leaders practice patience, reminding themselves to wait and observe, remembering that there's always more going on in a group than we're consciously aware of.

DIANE DREHER

Never dump a good idea on a conference table. It will belong to the conference.

JANE TRAHEY

Networking

A leader does not learn and grow in isolation. Women moving into leadership need to seek support from others, using the socio-emotional, financial, psychological, and intellectual resources others can provide.

L O I S   B O R L A N D   H A R T

Networking helps you on your path to success. With networking you can get the information and the contacts you need to move forward with your plans.

R O B I N   B O W M A N

Networking . . . can change your whole way of thinking about what it takes to succeed in business. As a technique, it will introduce you to stimulating, knowledgeable allies you didn't know you had. As a process, it knows no limits—and neither will you if you use it to its fullest potential.

MARY SCOTT WELCH

A leader needs to be "up." A positive attitude is synonymous with leadership. She needs to be nourished to maintain this perspective and that is where the importance of associations comes in. A leader should be with those who motivate her, and in places where inspiration exists.

JUDY COLUMBUS

All leaders need someone to whom they can bare their souls, someone with whom they can share life's frustrations and celebrations.

DIANE DREHER

One way to find out the steps necessary to get to the next position you want is to ask people already there to tell you how they made it.

BARBARA PATTERSON, NANCY MEADOWS, CAROL DREGER

Women, when describing their roles in their organizations, usually referred to themselves as being in the middle of things. Not at the top, but in the center; not reaching down, but reaching out.

SALLY HELGESEN

If networks of women are formed, they should be job related and task related rather than female-concerns related. Personal networks for sociability in the context of a work organization would tend to promote the image of women contained in the temperamental model—that companies must compensate for women's deficiencies and bring them together for support because they could not make it on their own. But job-related task forces serve the social-psychological functions while reinforcing a more positive image of women.

ROSABETH MOSS KANTER

Entrepreneurs

W omen indeed know their place. It's at the helm of their very own companies.

J A N E A N   C H U N

G oing into business for yourself, becoming an entrepreneur, is the modern-day equivalent of pioneering on the old frontier.

P A U L A   N E L S O N

There are no magics or elves
Or timely godmothers to guide us.
We are lost, must
Wizard a track through our own screaming weed.

GWENDOLYN BROOKS

If you want easy, don't become an entrepreneur.

CAROL COLUMBUS-GREEN

I run my company according to feminine principles, principles of caring, making intuitive decisions, not getting hung up on hierarchy or all those dreadfully boring business-school management ideas; having a sense of work as being part of your life, not separate from it; putting your labor where your love is; being responsible to the world in how you use your profits; recognizing the bottom line should stay at the bottom.

ANITA RODDICK

It's a given that if you start your own business, you're going to be (1) in control of your destiny, and (2) real busy.

GEORGETTE MOSBACHER

You must—you absolutely must—possess what can only be called leadership: that rare-as-rubies personal force that can resolve the clash of issues and personalities, pull others along with you, induce them to see things your way, to work their heads off in your young firm's behalf.

PAULA NELSON

It had long since come to my attention that people of accomplishment rarely sat back and let things happen to them. They went out and happened to things.

ELINOR SMITH

We need many more intrepid women who set out to expand both their and our concepts of the world. . . . Enough with decorousness. Let us risk preconceptions and treasured philosophies, bodies and souls. Let us be big and bawdy and full of courage. Let's go.

LESLEY HAZLETON

An entrepreneur is someone willing to go out on a limb, having it cut off behind her, and discovering she had wings all the time.

LEIGH THOMAS

When I'm dead, I want people to say: "That woman made a difference." I don't want that to seem like a conceited remark because it's not meant that way. But I think we all have an obligation to make life a little better—and a little pleasanter—for others.

LILLIAN VERNON

I don't think I'm a risk-taker. I don't think any entrepreneur is. I think that's one of those myths of commerce. The new entrepreneur is more values-led: you do what looks risky to other people because that's what your convictions tell you to do. Other companies would say I'm taking risks, but that's my path— it doesn't feel like risk to me.

ANITA RODDICK

What I try to do is . . . say to the baseball player: "Have you ever thought about owning your own baseball team?" To the would-be astronaut I ask: "Have you thought about owning the firm that makes the rockets?" There's not enough attention focused on entrepreneurship as a viable career.

HAZEL A. KING

We gain energy from being free to do those things we chose to do. We never tire when we are working on our projects.

ALEXANDRA STODDARD

The Orderly Office

The average executive wastes forty-five minutes each day searching for something lost on a desk, according to *Executive Female* magazine.

CONNIE GLASER AND
BARBARA STEINBERG SMALLEY

If we do not eliminate the clutter, the clutter will eliminate us.

PRISCILLA ELFREY

Carelessness with details sinks more careers than anyone will admit.

LOIS WYSE

Disorganization is neither in your fate nor in your genes. The ability to make sense of random data is a fundamental human attribute.

STEPHANIE WINSTON

Every hour has its immediate duty, its special injunction which dominates all others.

MARGUERITE YOURCENAR

I learned that in dealing with things, you spent much more time and energy in dealing with people than in dealing with things.

BUWEI YANG CHAO

Order is not an end in itself. Order is whatever helps you to function effectively—nothing more and nothing less.

STEPHANIE WINSTON

The manager with the in-basket problem does not yet understand that he must discipline himself to take care of activities that fail to excite him.

PRISCILLA ELFREY

Paper is perhaps the bane of our organizational existence, because paper is ubiquitous. Every day we are bombarded with, surrounded by, and submerged in an ever-increasing influx of printed material.

STEPHANIE WINSTON

Filing is concerned with the past; anything you actually need to see again has to do with the future.

KATHARINE WHITEHORN

Forget what organization experts tell you. Read it once, and if it has anything to do with you, *keep it in a file at home*. You will be very happy that you did.

KAREN RANDALL

Forget about remembering. The cost of forgetting is too high—write it down. And keep track of everything.

STEPHANIE WINSTON

It is said that the world is divided into two groups of people: those who have lost data, and those who are about to.

STEPHANIE WINSTON

First things first, second things never.

SHIRLEY CONRAN

The trouble with organizing a thing is that pretty soon folks get to paying more attention to the organization than to what they're organized for.

LAURA INGALLS WILDER

Disorder can play a critical role in giving birth to new, higher forms of order.

MARGARET J. WHEATLEY

Getting organized is not an end in itself; it is a means to get where you want to be.

STEPHANIE WINSTON

Interruptions

Have you ever noticed that life consists mostly of interruptions, with occasional spells of rush work in between?

BUWEI YANG CHAO

Studies indicate that the average manager is interrupted *every eight minutes*!

CONNIE GLASER AND
BARBARA STEINBERG SMALLEY

Successful leaders develop effective strategies for maintaining their boundaries. . . . Most time bandits don't know any better. And being a time bandit is a matter of context. One person's time bandit is another person's pleasant diversion. . . . Instead of gritting our teeth to be polite and resenting the time bandit for holding us up, the best choice is to be honest. We cannot expect another person to honor our needs unless we affirm them ourselves.

DIANE DREHER

Contacts with colleagues, staff, and clients are a necessary and legitimate part of doing business. The trick is not getting bogged down with inopportune, unscheduled chats in the hallway or on the phone.

STEPHANIE WINSTON

I'm always aware that I risk being taken for a neurasthenic prima donna when I explain to someone who wants "just a little" of my time that five minutes of the wrong kind of distraction can ruin a working day.

GAIL GODWIN

Patience ceases to be a virtue when it permits others to waste our time.

PAULINE M. SCHMIDT

Give yourself the gift of *uninterrupted time*. It can be the first hour of your day. Or the last hour. A lunch hour. You want time free from phone calls, visitors, mail, things to read. Unplug the phone if you have to. Lock your door. Put a sign on it that warns people of the consequences of entering. Do what you have to and watch the results. One hour of uninterrupted time can double a person's productivity for the day.

GERALDINE A. LARKIN

Women aren't trying to do too much.
Women have too much to do.

MARY KAY BLAKELY

I must govern the clock, not be governed by it.

GOLDA MEIR

I am a member of a small, nearly extinct
minority group, a kind of urban lost tribe who insist,
in the face of all evidence to the contrary, on the
sanctity of being on time. Which is to say that we
On-timers are compulsively, unfashionably prompt,
that there are only handfuls of us in any given city and,
unfortunately, we never seem to have appointments
with each other.

ELLEN GOODMAN

I never look at my watch if I'm talking with someone. I think that's such an insulting gesture! It suggests you're trying to gauge whether you think what they're saying is worth your time. Rushing is no way to bring out what's best in people, and I'm always looking for the best. That's what's ultimately behind my determination to take my time.

FRANCES HESSELBEIN

We have as much time as we need.

MELODY BEATTIE

Our perception that we have "no time" is one of the distinctive marks of modern Western culture.

MARGARET VISSER

I yield to no one in my admiration for the office as a social center, but it's no place actually to get any work done.

KATHARINE WHITEHORN

The very instrument that was supposed to be the greatest time-saver in our history has turned into the biggest time-waster. The telephone causes more interruption and generates more stress than anything else in our business environment.

CONNIE GLASER AND
BARBARA STEINBERG SMALLEY

The telephone exercises a terrible tyranny on most of us.

PRISCILLA ELFREY

 A ringing telephone is the insistent summons of modern life, and the decision not to take a call requires fortitude.

STEPHANIE WINSTON

 I've learned that by returning my calls between 11:00 A.M. and noon and 4:00 and 5:00 P.M. I can keep them short and to the point because people are either hungry and starting to think about lunch or they are trying to gear down at the end of the day.

GERALDINE A. LARKIN

 The interruptions of the telephone seem to us to waste half the life of the ordinary American engaged in public or private business; he has seldom half an hour consecutively at his own disposal—a telephone is a veritable *time scatterer*.

BEATRICE WEBB

Oh, how often I wished that Thomas A. Watson had laid a restraining hand on A.G. Bell's arm and had said to him, "Let's not and say we did."

JEAN MERCIER

At the end of every year, I add up the time that I have spent on the phone on hold and subtract it from my age. I don't count that time as really living. I spend more and more time on hold each year. By the time I die, I'm going to be quite young.

RITA RUDNER

Hi, this is Sylvia. I'm not at home right now, so when you hear the beep . . . hang up.

NICOLE HOLLANDER

Taking Care of Yourself

If you don't make time to take care of yourself, who will? Companies today need employees with quick minds, unique ideas, and the physical energy to put them together.

CONNIE PODESTA AND JEAN GATZ

First of my own personal requirements is inner calm. This, I think, is an essential. One of the secrets of using your time well is to gain a certain ability to maintain peace within yourself so that much can go on around you and you can stay calm inside.

ELEANOR ROOSEVELT

I get a massage almost every week, no matter where I am. I eat a healthy diet, I schedule time alone, and if I get to a point where I feel I need a block of time and I don't have it, I'll cancel. In general, I really listen to my body and pay attention to my needs.

ANNE WILSON SCHAEF

Others will survive even if we are not there taking care of them. I found out that I feel so much better when I take an hour a day, just to take care of me and love myself. It keeps me from feeling so put upon by everything and everybody and helps me get through the day. By taking my hour early in the morning, I feel like I get my love first and I get it when I am at my best.

BYLLYE AVERY

I used to have a sign on my desk at Columbia that said, "Breathe." So whenever there was one of those moments where I was faced with bad news or somebody was screaming at me—which happened more often than I can possibly tell you—I took deep breaths a lot.

D A W N   S T E E L

Are you taking time—making time—for fun and relaxation? . . . The word "recreation" divided into two parts becomes "re-creation." And that's just what we do when we spend time doing something we enjoy. Recreation helps us charge our batteries, re-create our energy, and continue to give our best at work.

C O N N I E   P O D E S T A   A N D   J E A N   G A T Z

I am convinced that there are times in every-body's experience when there is so much to be done, that the only way to do it is to sit down and do nothing.

F A N N Y   F E R N

Why should we need extra time in which to enjoy ourselves? If we expect to enjoy our life, we will have to learn to be joyful in all of it, not just at stated intervals when we can get time or when we have nothing else to do.

LAURA INGALLS WILDER

When you spend the day at a motivation workshop with a hotshot sent in from Phoenix with attaché case, jokes and uplifting statements, this is a tremendous upper—for about 24 hours. What is more important is the ability to refresh and elevate yourself and your thinking on a daily basis. You will find that your spirit can be contagious.

JUDY COLUMBUS

I had learned how to nurture myself, so besides hearing a critical voice, I had another voice inside me that said, I believe in you. Whatever you do is fine.

LAUREL KING

A constant tension exists between an individual's interests, personal needs, and skills, and what the organization requires of her. We've all asked ourselves, How much of my own agenda should I sacrifice in order to help the rest of the staff meet the company's goals?

PAT HEIM

The minute you settle for less than you deserve, you get even less than you settled for.

MAUREEN DOWD

You're never too young or too old to make your own kind of mark in your own kind of time. You're never the wrong age to release the power within you to create the life you deserve.

GEORGETTE MOSBACHER

Women for the most part don't look at life like a candy store. And they *should*. The first thing you need to do is to understand that everything is available to you, if you know what you want.

PAT HARRISON

Work, community, your own life—these have to be tied together. If you don't bring your whole self to a problem, then you're not going to be much of a problem solver, because you're not going to be giving the best parts of your mind to thinking.

DOROTHY BRUNSON

While our mental capabilities will help determine how long we stay employed, our physical well-being will help determine whether we can work to our full potential. Staying healthy should be an important priority for your personal and professional security and success. Creativity, energy, flexibility, confidence, and enthusiasm all come more easily from a well-rested, well-fed, and healthy body.

CONNIE PODESTA AND JEAN GATZ

Women . . . are virtual responsibility magnets. We don't make these decisions consciously or deliberately, but out of the fear that if we don't act on a need, it will never get resolved. . . . But we fail to realize that once we become responsible for something, we may be responsible to it forever.

PAT HEIM

In a society that judges self-worth on productivity, it's no wonder we fall prey to the misconception that the more we do, the more we're worth.

ELLEN SUE STERN

Each moment in time we have it all, even when we think we don't.

MELODY BEATTIE

Don't fool yourself that you are going to have it all. You are not. Psychologically, having it all is not even a valid concept. The marvelous thing about human beings is that we are perpetually reaching for the stars. The more we have, the more we want. And for this reason, we never have it all.

JOYCE BROTHERS

The *new* mystique is that women can have it all. There's a whole new generation of women today, flogging themselves to compete for success according to the male model—in a work world structured for men with wives to handle the details of life.

BETTY FRIEDAN

Most of us have trouble juggling. The woman who says that she doesn't is someone whom I admire but have never met.

BARBARA WALTERS

Total commitment to family and total commitment to career is possible, but fatiguing.

MURIEL FOX

I am not really sure that it is possible for most of us to fuse the personal and professional into one smooth, charming, comfortable, and competent whole—doing everything our mothers did, and everything our fathers did as well.

HILARY COSELL

What a denial of our humanity that at the centers of power, where decisions are made, there is no room for nurturing, for love, and children. There is more to life than the "inhuman" work place. It is terrible that many men do not know that: it is a tragedy if women follow them.

DORA RUSSELL

Leveling the Playing Field

W omen, with few exceptions, have had no place in history as leaders.

K A R I N   K L E N K E

T here is a vast arsenal of resistance to the idea of women as bosses. . . . The usual feelings of competitiveness aroused when a new person wins out are multiplied a thousandfold when that new person happens to be a woman.

J A N I C E   L A R O U C H E   A N D   R E G I N A   R Y A N

The more closed the circle, the more difficult it is for "outsiders" to break in. Their very difficulty in entering may be taken as a sign of incompetence, a sign that the insiders were right to close their ranks.

ROSABETH MOSS KANTER

There's plenty of room at the top, but there's no room to sit down.

HELEN DOWNEY

Because I am a woman I must make unusual efforts to succeed. If I fail, no one will say, "She doesn't have what it takes." They will say, "Women don't have what it takes."

CLARE BOOTHE LUCE

It is common to hear dedicated working women say they have to be twice as intelligent, three times as industrious, four times as enthusiastic, and work for half the money paid their male counterparts. Even then they may not be taken seriously. Many women feel that no matter how excellent their qualifications, the rise into management is blocked.

ELEANOR BRANTLEY SCHWARTZ

The higher a woman moves up in the work world, the more likely she is to be entirely surrounded by men. She feels conspicuous, and she is. Whatever she does is apt to be judged in terms of her womanness. If she succeeds it's because she's different from most women; if she fails it's because she's just like a woman.

MARY SCOTT WELCH

Women are penalized both for deviating from the masculine norm and for appearing to be masculine. When women try to establish their competence, they are scrutinized for evidence that they lack masculine (instrumental) characteristics as well as for signs that they no longer possess female (expressive) ones. They are taken to fail, in other words, both as a male and as a female.

KATHLEEN HALL JAMIESON

So a girl is damned if she does, damned if she doesn't. If she refuses to talk like a lady, she is ridiculed and subjected to criticism as unfeminine; if she does learn, she is ridiculed as unable to think clearly, unable to take part in a serious discussion: in some sense, as less than fully human. These two choices which a woman has—to be less than a woman or less than a person—are highly painful.

ROBIN LAKOFF

Those power styles and strategies that are most associated with being perceived as powerful and competent, with being effective or persuasive, are also associated with being masculine. . . . The evidence suggests that both masculine and feminine styles may be effective if used by men, but masculine styles are not effective when used by women. . . . Women have the choice of using power in an indirect (manipulative) way and risking either being ineffective or unrecognized, or using direct styles and risking being both ineffective and disliked.

ANN HARRIMAN

Women are called difficult and tough when (1) we negotiate the best deal, (2) we are perfectionists in doing our job, (3) we are willing to work harder and longer than men are willing to, and (4) when we question anything—*anything*—that someone else is doing, particularly if that someone is a man.

GEORGETTE MOSBACHER

Women are operating in institutions created by men, and that is like being in another culture, a foreign country. There are some male behavioral patterns that women have not grown up with. It is hard for women to become part of the informal power networks in the company. Men are in them naturally, and the information and reinforcement they receive are essential to moving ahead. Women are thus held to a difficult standard. They are expected to strike exactly the right balance between being aggressive and tough-minded on the one hand and being feminine on the other. And they find it's often a no-win situation.

BARBARA H. FRANKIN

To be successful, a woman has to be much better at her job than a man.

GOLDA MEIR

If there is one fact of corporate life which women of all philosophical persuasions seem to agree on, it is that women must work harder as a group than men to succeed within management. Regardless of the stories one may hear about unqualified women who are allegedly promoted to satisfy quotas, most women managers still believe that, as a group, they are moving up the hard way—by working diligently to prove their competence again and again.

MARILYN LODEN

Stories told around the water-cooler as well as statistics confirm that a man's competence is more likely to be presupposed, a woman's questioned.

KATHLEEN HALL JAMIESON

A woman's success is more likely to be explained by external factors like luck or ease of task, or by high effort, an internal but unstable factor, whereas a man's success is more likely to be attributed to high ability. The reverse is true for explanations of failure; men are said to fail because of hard luck, a hard task, or low effort, whereas women are said to fail because of low ability.

BERNICE LOTT

Research has shown that men attribute their success to ability; both men and women in research studies attribute women's successes to luck. If we believe that women succeed only by chance, by extension we also believe that women are incapable of creating success.

ROBIN BOWMAN

Other problems confront women in power. One is fine but two's a crowd seems to be an unspoken rule when the one wears a skirt. And those in authority have found ways to reward women for excluding others of their kind.

KATHLEEN HALL JAMIESON

Having the right image—the way people see you—is crucial to getting what you want from work: respect, raises, promotions, good working relationships, and an easier time of it all around. This holds for everyone in the workplace, but the "right" image is particularly essential for women because they have to overcome the handicap of being the "wrong" sex.

JANICE LAROUCHE AND REGINA RYAN

Men and women can learn valuable lessons of leadership from each other in today's workplace. Together as men and women we can create meaningful synergy at work if we value the specific orientations we bring. Most importantly, if as individuals, whether male or female, we become *fully who we are* we will incorporate those parts of ourselves that have been repressed by social conditioning.

DELORESE AMBROSE

Men and women . . . need and want recognition of their value and uniqueness. The goal is not to make women more like men, or men more like women, but for everyone to become most like themselves.

ELEANOR BRANTLEY SCHWARTZ

The truth is that distinctions between how men and women project management and leadership qualities are narrowing. The real problem lies with the fact that, as a female New York banker states, "there is a very narrow band of 'acceptable' behavior, which is a blend of men's and women's values." In an increasingly diverse work force, this narrow band must expand for both men and women, and for the ultimate productivity of American businesses.

DAWN-MARIE DRISCOLL AND
CAROL R. GOLDBERG

There do appear to be more differences between women managers and nonmanagers than there are between women and men managers.

ANN HARRIMAN

I don't expend mental energy trying to figure out what's masculine or feminine. I don't think about it. And I think I'm freer not thinking about it. There is some correlation to physiology, but it's not complete, and there's no need to strain it. The natural differences between men and women will maintain themselves. People don't have to get uptight and force themselves for ideological reasons to be "masculine" or "feminine." I disapprove of social coercion in that direction. If it's natural and biologically inevitable, it'll stand up by itself. And if it's not natural, then who needs it?

MARION EDEY

We still think of a powerful man as a born leader and a powerful woman as an anomaly.

MARGARET ATWOOD

Some leaders are born women.

GERALDINE A. FERRARO

There are apparently no gender differences between women and men in terms of leadership style. . . . What differences appear to exist seem to disappear when other variables are taken into account. . . . Even though the preponderance of the evidence shows scant differences at most, stereotypes continue to favor the "male is normal" model of leadership. . . . The most encouraging implication from the research is that stereotypes tend to become less important as experience increases.

Ann Harriman

There are certain qualities—courage, and character, and vitality, *a kind of belonging to oneself*—which make men seem manlier and women seem womanlier, in the way that certain chemicals make blue liquids bluer and red liquids redder. Vitality looks very masculine on a man, very feminine on a woman; very sexy either way.

Susan Edmiston

Even the new feminist research on sex-role socialization and sex differences has sometimes had the unfortunate consequence of creating a new set of stereotypes about what women feel and how women behave. Despite the large amount of overlap between the sexes in most research, the tendency to label and polarize and thus to exaggerate differences remains in much reporting of data, which may, for example, report the mean scores of male and female populations but not the degree of overlap.

ROSABETH MOSS KANTER

Empirical evidence of female-male differences in leader behaviors, leadership styles, and evaluations of female and male leaders is fragile at best. . . . In contrast to popular writers, leadership researchers generally seem to agree that there are few and negligible gender differences in actual leader behavior. Moreover, the scientific evidence fails to support the notion of a distinctive "feminine" leadership style portrayed by the popular literature.

KARIN KLENKE

The difference between men and women is that women seek power in order to address issues, while men address issues in order to seek power.

KATHLEEN BROWN

Whether there are innately female leadership styles . . . is not really the right question. It is more important to ask why there has been so little attention paid to women leaders over the years as well as why the styles of leading more often exhibited by women are particularly useful at this critical moment in history. The empowering, cooperative approaches most often associated with women are not exclusively female terrain. If we see these as crucial models for leadership in the twenty-first century, then we do not want only women to adopt them.

CHARLOTTE BUNCH

The media want [nontraditional managers] for stories and profiles. Social scientists want them for research projects. Other men of color or women, with ambitions of their own, want them as role models and regularly call them for advice or favors. Nonprofit organizations ask them to speak at conventions. Their bosses sometimes nudge them to serve on committees and task forces as the ranking woman or person of color to represent that point of view. Employee groups beckon them to mentor others of the same sex or ethnicity. Top management may want their help in recruiting other nontraditional employees. The amount of necessary "volunteerism" within and outside the organization escalates for nontraditional managers, who must also continue to do their jobs in a consistently outstanding fashion to stay in good stead with their bosses.

ANN M. MORRISON

Women tend not to rise to their level of incompetency in business, as suggested by the Peter Principle, because women are not automatically promoted as men are.

MARCILLE GRAY WILLIAMS

Women in leadership roles share many of the structural characteristics of tokens: they are highly visible, public individuals who attract attention with anything they do; as such, they are stand-ins for all women, symbols of how women behave and perform as leaders. . . . Token leaders find themselves in the organizational limelight; their actions and moves are constantly scrutinized, and they are faced with pressures that result from the application of performance standards that are only applicable to tokens. Many token women have reported that they must work twice as hard as their male colleagues to be considered competent.

KARIN KLENKE

Women do not have to depend on men in order to advance in leadership. Women in the United States would not be able to vote today if they waited for men to give them the vote. It is the same for feminine leadership in any field. Women have to work for what they believe in and cause it to happen. The problems that men have in accepting women will be overcome by women, not by men.

SYLVIA BUSHELL

What business needs now is exactly what women are able to provide, and at the very time when women are surging into the work force. But perhaps even more important than work force numbers is the fact that women . . . are just now beginning to assume positions of leadership, which give them the scope to create and reinforce the trends toward change. The confluence is fortunate, an alignment that gives women unique opportunities to assist in the continuing transformation of the workplace.

SALLY HELGESEN

Women and people of color often have to be careful about how they convey their passion and conviction, particularly with what are considered stereotypically female or minority issues. Often expressions of passion in white men are lauded, while similar passion is often seen as emotionalism when it is expressed by women, or confrontation when it is expressed by men of color.

SARA E. MELÉNDEZ

Vision is the first important characteristic of leadership, and it can present an obstacle for people of color, women, individuals with disabilities, and others who are not cast in the traditional mold. Their ability to communicate their different vision will be their first major challenge.

SARA E. MELÉNDEZ

As women, Blacks, Hispanics, Asians, and American Indians began to move into the world of management, the emphasis was not on learning from them. Efforts focused, instead, on fitting minorities and women into what once was the domain of white men. These efforts almost totally missed the point by failing to take advantage of the new resources being brought to the management world. Interestingly, though, as affirmative action has gained ground, management theory and practice are expanding the concept of what makes a good manager. The new members of the workforce exhibit many of the behaviors that are being discussed and very tentatively tried out by managers.

ALICE G. SARGENT

The American women's movement, in the closing quarter of the twentieth century, began in the workplace. Twenty-five years later it is still a work in progress. Despite efforts to make them comprehensible, broad social movements do not proceed in neat and orderly fashion, participants marching single file, their eyes glued to the future. Such movements are ill-defined, contradictory, painful, exhilarating. Like biological evolution, social processes advance and retreat in fits and starts, sometimes so incrementally as to seem nonexistent. But change is inexorable, and once unleashed cannot be contained. The movement of women today is no exception. At different speeds, in different ways, it is a worldwide happening. . . . Change happens in spirals, not cycles, and there is no going back.

SARA ANN FRIEDMAN

Library of Congress Cataloging-in-Publication Data

Maggio, Rosalie
      An impulse to soar : quotations by women on leadership / compiled by
   Rosalie Maggio.
           p.   cm.
      ISBN 0-7352-0014-9 (cloth)
      1. Leadership—Quotations, maxims, etc.   2. Women—Quotations,
   maxims, etc.   I. Title.
   PN6084.L15M34   1998
   303.3'4—dc21   98-17897
                                                                        CIP

ISBN 0-7352-0014-9

Text design: *Suzanne Behnke*

Excerpts from *The New Beacon Book of Quotations by Women*
(Boston: Beacon Press, 1996) are reprinted with permission.

PRENTICE HALL PRESS
Paramus, NJ 07652

A Simon & Schuster Company

On the World Wide Web at http://www.phdirect.com

Prentice Hall International (UK) Limited, *London*
Prentice Hall of Australia Pty. Limited, *Sydney*
Prentice Hall of Canada, Inc., *Toronto*
Prentice Hall Hispanoamericana, S.A., *Mexico*
Prentice Hall of India Private Limited, *New Delhi*
Prentice Hall of Japan, Inc., *Tokyo*
Simon & Schuster Asia Pte. Ltd., *Singapore*
Editora Prentice Hall do Brasil, Ltda., *Rio de Janeiro*

BAKER & TAYLOR